From Screen to Theme

A Guide to Disney Animated Film References Found Throughout the Walt Disney World® Resort

Brent Dodge

www.fromscreentotheme.com

First published by Dog Ear Publishing
4010 W. 86th Street, Ste H
Indianapolis, IN 46268
www.dogearpublishing.net

ISBN: 978-160844-408-3

This book is printed on acid-free paper.

Printed in the United States of America

Dedication

I am going to dedicate it to several people:

To my parents, who have always been supportive. Thank you for putting up with my useless Disney knowledge for years and for taking me to Walt Disney World several times while growing up.

To my three brothers. Thank you for not just being great brothers but great friends as well. If it weren't for the three of you this book would not be a reality. Thank you to Travis for helping me with the editing, Justin for being my webmaster, and Tyler for helping me research the book.

To my Grandparents. Without your continued support and help throughout life I know I would not be who I am today. You have set a great example to me on how to live life. I feel extremely lucky to have such wonderful grandparents and am extremely thankful for all of you.

Especially to my Grandma Dodge, who not only shared a love of Disney with me, but was the first person I ever confided in about my dream of someday working at Walt Disney World. I count myself lucky every day knowing that you saw me live out my greatest dream. We all love and miss you every day.

Acknowledgements

This book would not be a reality without the support and patience of several people. First off, I would like to thank the many Cast Members (past, present, and future) that put up with my constant questions during my research trips and phone calls. Not only have you done your best to answer my every question, but you make everyone's visits to Walt Disney World extraordinary. Walt Disney World is what it is because of you.

I would also like to thank my fellow online "Disney nerds," especially the W.E.D.friends. Your constant support and encouragement is unbelievable. Thank you for believing in a guy who most of you have never met. I hope this book is everything you dreamed it would be.

I would like to thank all of my friends who have joined me on my many research trips, especially Kyle, Kathryn, Erin, Jolie, and Amanda. Not only did each of you make great travel buddies, but you listened to me blab on for days about Disney. You are all amazing!

Finally, I would like to thank my family for their constant support. You have encouraged me every step of the way (even though I'm sure part of that was to keep me out of your sight). Thank you especially to Travis for helping with the editing, Justin for helping with the website, Tyler for helping with the research, and Mom and Pa (that's right, I said Pa) for the encouragement and support. I love you all and I hope I have made you proud.

Introduction

I would like to start by thanking you for picking up this book.

Like so many people, I have had a love of all things Disney for as long as I can remember. When I was three years old, I had two dreams. The first was to work at Walt Disney World and the second was to own Herbie the Love Bug. As I grew up, these two dreams never died and it resulted in a lot of (friendly) ridicule from family and friends. They couldn't believe I could watch the Disney movies over and over again or want to visit Walt Disney World every chance I had.

Fortunately, my love of Disney never faded. When I was in college, I was accepted into the Walt Disney World College Program where I had the chance to live out one of my childhood dreams. While working as a custodian in Fantasyland, a guest once approached me about where he could find "Peter Pan" references. After explaining every reference in all the parks and Downtown Disney, he pointed out that there really should be a book dedicated to this subject. Being the genius I am, I ignored his idea and continued sweeping the streets of Fantasyland.

While watching the 3 o'clock parade a few months later, I noticed that Bernard and Bianca, from "The Rescuers," were on Aladdin's float, and I became obsessed with trying to find other references to "The Rescuers" movies in the parks. My roommate Kyle and I began looking at Walt Disney World in a whole new way as we searched for the tiny details the Imagineers had hidden throughout the parks for people like us to find. Unfortunately, I still didn't think about writing a book.

Three years later while student teaching, the students were having rest time and watching "Robin Hood." While watching the film, I tried to figure out where Robin Hood references could be found throughout the Walt Disney World® Resort. I quickly remembered what my Peter Pan buddy had told me years before, and within a few days I had an entire notebook filled with references.

A brand new dream was born. I was going to share all of the "useless" knowledge I had gained throughout the years about Disney movies and Walt Disney World and share it with people like you. I began to schedule trips to Walt Disney World (I know, research is brutal, right?) and pretty soon I had an almost 400 page book written about references to the Disney animated films, live action films, classic characters, and short cartoons.

I realized a 400 page guide book was too much to carry around the parks and eventually made the decision to turn the one rather large book into two smaller books. The first one, the one you are reading right now, focuses around the animated films only, while the second book, which is expected to be out in Fall 2010, focuses around the live action films, classic characters, and short cartoons.

I hope you enjoy finding these references as much as I have!

Brent Dodge

P.S. For those of you wondering, I eventually bought "Herbie."

How the book is organized

Unlike most guides to Walt Disney World, From Screen to Theme doesn't focus around individual parks, but individual movies. This gives you the opportunity to choose the film(s) you want to concentrate on during your visit. Each specific chapter begins with a brief recap of the film followed by a mixture of fun facts, references to the film, and locations of character meet and greets for that particular film.

If you are in a specific section of Walt Disney World and are curious which movies have references in the area, simply turn to the Index in the back of the book to discover which pages you need to go to for your next reference. If you cannot find a specific area, attraction, restaurant, etc. in the Index, that means there has yet to be a discovered reference for an animated film in that area.

The references in this book range from extremely obvious (yes, Peter Pan's Flight is based off of "Peter Pan") to some extremely hidden finds (one of the rafts on Kali River Rapids has a nod to a character from "The Jungle Book"). Unless you are staying for a lengthy visit, you will most likely not be able to find every reference in this book during your stay. Due to this, I suggest selecting a few films to concentrate on during your visit. While searching for these references, you are bound to find references to other films in the process!

Not all of the Disney animated films have references in the parks. "The Black Cauldron," "The Great Mouse Detective," "Home on the Range," and "Bolt" currently do not have any references found within Walt Disney World. In addition, if a reference to a film has not been present for at least nine months or has a strong possibility of changing, it is also not included in the book. For instance, at the time of printing, you could meet Russell, Dug, and Carl Fredrickson from "Up" in the Animation Courtyard. Due to the fact this reference will likely disappear in the near future, it is not included.

Walt Disney World is constantly changing on a daily basis. Due to this, some of the references found within this book may disappear by the time of your next visit arrives. At the same time, additional references may suddenly appear in the parks as well! If you find a new reference, feel free to share it with me and your fellow readers at www.fromscreentotheme.com so others can look for it on their next visit. At the same time, as soon as I can confirm a reference in the park has disappeared, I will update www.fromscreentotheme. com so you will not waste your time searching for it during your next visit.

Good luck in your search!

"Snow White and the Seven Dwarfs"

Released: December 21, 1937

The film in three paragraphs:

After Snow White's mother died, her father married the first of many "evil stepmothers" in Disney history. Each day her stepmother would go before her Magic Mirror and ask, "Magic mirror, on the wall, who is the fairest one of all?" After replying Snow White, the Queen becomes outraged and orders a huntsman to take Snow White in the woods and kill her. The huntsman, unable to commit the crime, tells Snow White to run away and he returns with a pig's heart to show the Queen that Snow White is dead.

Meanwhile, some forest animals lead Snow White to the cottage of the Seven Dwarfs. Snow White tidies up the cottage and falls asleep. The Dwarfs are startled when they find her at first, but agree they should let her stay. Back at the castle, the Queen asks the mirror the ever popular question again, to which he responds that Snow White is still the fairest in the land. The Queen turns herself into an old hag and, with a poisoned apple in hand, sets off to kill Snow White herself.

While the Dwarfs are at their mine, the old Queen, disguised as the old hag, arrives at the cottage and explains to Snow White that the apple is a magic wishing apple. Snow White bites it and falls into a deep sleep. The Dwarfs return home and chase the old hag to the top of a cliff where she falls to her death. Several months later, the Prince finds Snow White, kisses her, and she awakens. The two ride off and live happily ever after.

Magic Kingdom

Starting off in the Magic Kingdom, you can find your first references on **Main Street, USA.**

1) The first references are located in **Exposition Hall**, the first building on your right after passing under the Walt Disney World Railroad tracks. You can have your picture taken with a diorama of Snow White and the Seven Dwarfs from the "Silly Song" scene of the film in the back room of the shop. There is room between Sneezy and Dopey allowing you to become the eighth dwarf.

2) The back wall of the same room in **Exposition Hall** chronicles the Milestones in Disney Animation. The mural contains a picture of the Prince kissing Snow White and a semi-transparent Grumpy. There is also a description worth reading that explains why Snow White is considered a milestone in Disney animation history.

3) The **Emporium** contains the next reference on Main Street, USA. One of the corner windows facing Town Square shows Snow White and all Seven Dwarfs during the "Silly Song" scene of the film, depicted by miniature models.

When you have finished finding your references on Main Street, USA, stop by **Fantasyland** for your next three references!

4) **Character Meet and Greet alert!** A great place to meet Snow White is at **Cinderella's Royal Table**, the restaurant located inside the castle, during the **Once Upon a Time Character Breakfast**. This is a very popular breakfast, so make reservations in advance to guarantee a seat at this amazing Character breakfast.

5) After entering Fantasyland through the castle, you can find **Snow White's Scary Adventures** on your right hand side. While waiting in line, look at both the mural on the back wall and the ride cars, which are actually mine cars. If you look at the front of each mine car, you will notice that each car is named after a different dwarf. You can find all the

main characters and scenes from the film throughout the attraction.

Fun Fact: Originally Snow White's Scary Adventures did not feature the fair princess! This was due to the fact that you, the rider, were playing the part of Snow White. However, too many guests were confused and kept wondering where Snow White was so Disney decided to add her to the attraction.

6) Just past the ride on your right hand side is a small gift shop dedicated to the film called **Seven Dwarfs Mining Co.** You can find all of your favorite Dwarfs on the main sign above the shop. The inside of the shop is themed to look like the Dwarf's mine.

Fun Fact: Did you know Dopey is the only Dwarf that does not talk? According to Happy, "He never tried." He is also the only Dwarf that has no facial hair.

The remaining references to Snow White and the Seven Dwarfs in the Magic Kingdom take place during the **Fireworks, Parades, and Shows.** Times Guides are available throughout the park and will let you know when you can find each of the following references.

7) During the **Dream Along With Mickey** show, one of the main characters talks about how she wishes she was a princess. After these words are spoken, Snow White and her Prince come out and dance on stage.

8) The Queen makes an appearance during **SpectroMagic** on a float with Captain Hook. You can find Dopey hanging out with Geppetto and Pinocchio a few floats behind her, while Snow White and the remaining Dwarfs follow behind to close out the parade.

9) The final references in the Magic Kingdom to Snow White occur during **"Wishes,"** a not to be missed fireworks show. You can hear several Disney characters make wishes during the show including Snow White. However, the biggest reference to the film comes later in the show when The Queen shows up to ruin the fun. During the scene, The Queen beckons the Magic Mirror to come forth. If you are in front of the castle, which is recommended, make sure you take note that the two sections of the castle on the lower half near the tunnel actually display the Magic Mirror, face and all!

Epcot

The only two references at Epcot can be found in **World Showcase.**

10) **Character Meet and Greet Alert!** You can meet Snow White at the **Princess Storybook Breakfast** at **Akershus,** a sit down restaurant in **Norway.** This is a popular breakfast so make sure you book your reservations as far in advance as possible.

11) **Character Meet and Greet Alert!** At times throughout the day, you can meet Snow White and Dopey in **Germany** near her wishing well. On very rare occasions, you can actually find all Seven Dwarfs walking around the Germany pavilion together. Take note that this is an extremely rare opportunity.

Disney's Hollywood Studios

Disney's Hollywood Studios contains several references to Snow White and the Seven Dwarfs starting on **Hollywood Boulevard.**

12) At the end of **The Great Movie Ride,** you will watch several clips from various films including a quick clip from Snow White and the Seven Dwarfs.

13) Just before you enter the **Animation Courtyard** from Hollywood Boulevard, make sure you take a look at the arch you pass under. Near the top of the arch is a carving of Carthay Circle Theatre, the theatre where Snow White and the Seven Dwarfs premiered.

14) If you listen closely, you will realize there are songs playing everywhere throughout Walt Disney World. The **Animation Courtyard** is no different. In the area leading up to The Magic of Disney Animation, you can hear the upbeat "Whistle While You Work" at various times throughout the day.

15) While waiting in line for **The Magic of Disney Animation**, you can find several concept sketches on the walls from various Disney films. One sketch shows the Prince at the beginning of the film as he listens to Snow White's "I'm Wishing" song. If the area is roped off, ask a Cast Member if you can take a look at the pictures. The majority of the time they are more than happy to let you.

16) Just after entering **The Magic of Disney Animation**, you will be seated in a small theatre. The screen behind the host will show a variety of Disney animated characters during the opening comments. Watch closely for Snow White in one clip and all Seven Dwarfs in another.

17) Have you ever wanted to be the voice of a cartoon character? What about being the voice for The Seven Dwarfs? While in the **Magic of Disney Animation** building, you can! Stop by the interactive game titled, "**The Sound Stage**" and select the Sing option. You can then put your voice into the song "Heigh-Ho!"

18) The artwork in the Oscar room of **The Magic of Disney Animation** building is primarily focused around Snow White and the Seven Dwarfs.

19) Look at the pictures above some of the displays in the shop **In Character** to find "pencil" sketches of Snow White that show the correct way to draw her!

20) While watching the film, **One Man's Dream**, you can see several quick scenes from various Disney films. There is a rather large portion, however, that focuses around Snow White and the Seven Dwarfs. During this segment, you can find Snow White, the old hag, the Prince, all Seven Dwarfs during the "Heigh Ho!" scene, Happy dancing, and a few other clips from the early stages of animation for the film.

Fun Fact: Although "One Man's Dream" makes it look like Walt Disney provided the voice of the Queen, he actually did not. Lucille La Verne was the actual provider of the voice. Rumor has it that she produced the voice of the Hag so perfectly only after removing her false teeth.

21) If you head into the restaurant **Hollywood & Vine**, you will find a mural on the wall. The center of this mural shows the famous Carthay Circle Theatre where the film premiered.

22) While on **Sunset Boulevard**, stop by the connected stores **Sweet Spells** and **Villains In Vogue** and take a look at the walls to find a carving of the Queen. You can also find The Magic Mirror above some of the displays inside the shop. If you take a look at one of the windows on the outside of the shop, you can see the Queen as the old Hag with the Mirror in the background. This extremely detailed spot looks like her dungeon where she conjures up her spells.

23) Continue down Sunset Boulevard to the final shop on your right, just before the Theatre of the Stars, for your next reference. The sign outside the shop pointing towards the corner reads "Carthay Circle Theatre." The shop is actually called **Once Upon a Time** and does not have anything to

do with Snow White and the Seven Dwarfs, but it is a nice tribute to the theatre which premiered one of the most loved films of all time.

24) While walking into **Fantasmic!** you will pass several banners with different Disney characters on them, including one of the Queen as the Hag. You can also sit in her section which is marked off with the same picture at the top of the seats. The seats here do not provide the best viewing of the show, but it is still fun to have your picture taken with the sign!

25) During the "Dancing Bubbles" sequence of **Fantasmic!** you can find all seven dwarfs within their own bubbles while an instrumental version of "Heigh Ho!" is played.

26) During the "Princess Medley" segment of **Fantasmic!** you can find Snow White and her Prince dancing on their water float as a modern version of "Someday My Prince Will Come" plays on the speakers. Immediately after Snow White and her Prince are out of sight, the evil Queen takes center stage with the Magic Mirror on the water screens. It is during this scene that you can witness a live transformation of the Queen turning into the Hag.

27) During the finale of **Fantasmic!** you can usually find Snow White, the Prince, and all Seven Dwarfs on the steamboat.

Fun Fact: Did you know the first Disney character to ever speak in a feature length animated film was the evil Queen?

Downtown Disney

Your next stop for finding Snow White, seven men, and their forest friends is at **Downtown Disney**. The first group of references can be found on the **Marketplace** side of Downtown Disney.

28) One of the best themed shops on property, **Disney's Days of Christmas**, has several references to multiple Disney films that are all themed to the famous song 12 Days of Christmas. What would your true love give to you on the seventh day of Christmas? Seven Dwarfs a-mining of course! Upon the wall where the seventh day falls, you can find all seven dwarfs in their mine.

29) The next reference is outside of **Once Upon a Toy**. Make your way towards the back door near the fountains to find a picture of Snow White with five other Disney princesses in one of the windows.

30) What can be more picture perfect than a princess in a picture portrait? Located inside the **Marketplace's Guest Relations** is a framed picture of Snow White.

Fun Fact: There were several other Dwarfs that were being considered for the film. Some of their names include Shorty, Hoppy, Gloomy, Lazy, Puffy, and, my personal favorite, Flabby.

31) Enter **World of Disney** through the entrance below Mickey and Minnie. Once inside, go to the first room on your right hand side and look at the ceiling to find several Disney birds and other tree loving animals. If you look closely, you can find the doves that helped exchange Snow White and the Prince's first kiss. Now that's romantic!

32) Head through the "Bird Room" in **World of Disney**, enter the next room, and take a look at the mural behind the cash register to find Snow White washing the steps with her forest friends nearby.

33) There are several great references in the "Princess Hall" section of **World of Disney**. If you look above the exit, you will find a gigantic sign which reads, "Happily Ever After." On this sign is Snow White and seven other Disney

princesses. Turn towards the back of the store and look left to find a picture of Snow White and the Prince high on the wall.

34) If you head to the back of the same room in **World of Disney**, you can find several castles that are in stained glass windows. The one on the far right is Snow White's castle, which she shared with her stepmother, the evil Queen.

35) The final reference to Snow White and the Seven Dwarfs within **World of Disney** is in the "Villains Room." This room is located in the center of the back portion of the store. There are several villains' hands coming out of the walls in this room. The Old Hag's hand, with an apple of course, is one of the hands you can find here. Can you figure out who the other hands belong to?

36) The final reference in **Downtown Disney's Marketplace** can be found anywhere. As pointed out earlier, music is playing everywhere in Walt Disney World and, if you listen closely in this area, you can hear the "Mine Song/Heigh Ho." This is one of thirty-two songs that play in the area so the odds of hearing it within the first few songs are pretty slim.

For the final Snow White and the Seven Dwarfs reference in Downtown Disney, head over to **Downtown Disney's West Side**.

37) While walking the main pathway in Downtown Disney's West Side, you can find the **Candy Cauldron** on your left hand side. Above the entrance you can find our good friend, The Old Hag, lowering the ever famous apple into her potion. While inside the store, take a look below the cash register. The counter is a replica of the box the Huntsman was suppose to return Snow White's heart in. Don't worry as there is no pig's heart in sight!

Resorts

The final references to the film that started it all are found in **All-Star Movies**.

38) While in the **World Premiere** food court, you can find a poster for "Snow White and the Seven Dwarfs" on one of the walls.

39) While waiting for the buses at **All-Star Movies**, take a look at the windows behind you and next to the entrance of **Donald's Double Features** to find Snow White among several other characters.

"Pinocchio"

Released: February 7, 1940

The Film in Three Paragraphs

The story of Pinocchio focuses around dreams. The film begins with a very sad looking Jiminy Cricket singing the ever popular "When You Wish Upon a Star." He heads over to a lighted window and looks in to see Geppetto's house/work shop. Jiminy enters the house and sees that Geppetto has made a new puppet, Pinocchio. Before heading to bed that night, Geppetto wishes upon a star that his little wooden head, Pinocchio, could be a real boy.

That night, the Blue Fairy arrives and grants Geppetto's wish, but tells Pinocchio that if he wants to be a real boy, he must be brave, truthful, and unselfish. Jiminy Cricket is appointed Pinocchio's conscious. Although Pinocchio thinks it will be easy to go down the right path, he ends up trusting the wrong people. J. Worthington Foulfellow and his assistant Gideon convince him that first he should become an actor. Following that advice results in Pinocchio being mistreated by a puppet owner named Stromboli. Foulfellow and Gideon later convince Pinocchio to go to a place called Pleasure Island, where boys are turned into donkeys.

While Pinocchio travels down the wrong path, Geppetto searches for him, which results in him being swallowed by a whale named Monstro! Pinocchio enters the sea with hopes of saving his father. Pinocchio joins Geppetto in the belly of Monstro where the two build a fire to make Monstro sneeze Geppetto and Pinocchio out. After a struggle to get away, Geppetto finds his little Pinocchio dead. While Geppetto mourns Pinocchio, the Blue Fairy points out that Pinocchio was brave, truthful, and unselfish and turns him into a real boy.

Magic Kingdom

You can find your first few references to Pinocchio on **Main Street, USA**. No lie!

1) Your first reference to Pinocchio is in the back room of **Exposition Hall**. The back wall is devoted to the Milestones in Disney Animation. One of the pictures shows our little wooden head headed off to school with his ever popular conscience, Jiminy Cricket, in front of him.

2) **Character Meet and Greet Alert!** Throughout the day, you can find Geppetto, Pinocchio, Gideon, and Foulfellow at **Town Square**. All of these characters do not make appearances every day and the times typically vary from day to day so check with a cast member to find out when and where you should be to find each character.

3) The final reference to Pinocchio on Main Street is one of my favorites throughout all of Walt Disney World. If you head to the **Hub**, located at the end of Main Street, you can

find several small bronze statues of Disney characters including one of Pinocchio and Jiminy Cricket together.

Hi Diddle Dee Dee! It's Liberty Square for ye. Here you'll find a Christmas shop, lots of ghosts and a soda pop! That's right! While at the Hub and facing Cinderella Castle, take the path directly to the left of the castle and head into **Liberty Square**.

4) After walking across the bridge from Main Street, USA to Liberty Square, enter the first store on your left hand side, **Ye Olde Christmas Shoppe**. This store is actually separated into three different rooms. If you head into the middle room, you can find Pinocchio high on a shelf on the back wall. Sometimes the best way to see him is by standing as far back as possible.

Fantasyland is home to the largest structure on Walt Disney World property devoted to Pinocchio. Travel through the veranda between the Haunted Mansion and the Columbia Harbor House to the land where magic truly lives.

5) After entering Fantasyland from Liberty Square, you will pass It's a Small World on your left hand side. The restaurant next door is the **Pinocchio Village Haus**. If you look at the sign facing Dumbo, you can find Pinocchio! Go inside for some fun finds! Each room is themed around a different character from the film. They consist of Jiminy Cricket, Monstro, Figaro, Cleo, Geppetto, Stromboli, and the Blue Fairy. Interestingly, there is no room dedicated to Pinocchio himself.

Fun Fact: Unlike Disneyland, Disneyland Paris, and Tokyo Disneyland, Walt Disney World's Fantasyland does not have the ride Pinocchio's Daring Journey.

Continue walking through Fantasyland towards the Mad Tea Party. When you reach the Mad Tea Party, veer to the left and enter **Mickey's Toontown Fair** for your next Pinocchio reference.

6) Your destination in Toontown is **Minnie's Country House**, the first house on your left after Pete's Garage. Look closely at the pictures on the wall in Minnie's living room. In the far corner is a picture of Minnie bandaging up Mickey's dog Pluto. In the same picture, you can see Figaro pulling on one of Pluto's bandages.

Fun Fact: Even though Pinocchio was not the most popular film at the time, Figaro the cat went on to co-star as Minnie's pet cat in seven short cartoons with Pluto.

The remaining references for Pinocchio in the Magic Kingdom occur during the **Parades** and **Wishes**.

7) The **Celebrate A Dream Come True Parade** has several characters from Pinocchio. Gideon and Foulfellow walk in front of Pinocchio's float Behind them is Pinocchio front and center on his float along with Jiminy Cricket and Geppetto. If you are on the right hand side of the float, you will have a great chance to see Figaro trying to catch Cleo in her fishbowl.

8) Jiminy Cricket is the host of the night time spectaculars in the Magic Kingdom. The first one he hosts is **Spectro-Magic**. He introduces the show before the first float arrives. During the parade you will see Geppetto and Pinocchio on one of the last floats with Dopey. One of the best things to watch for during the parade is Jiminy Cricket. He is on the back of the final float. He is very small and easy to miss, but a great find.

9) As with SpectroMagic, Jiminy Cricket is also the host for **Wishes**, the amazing fireworks show that occurs nightly at the Magic Kingdom. He is actually the co-host of this show with The Blue Fairy. During the show, you can hear Pinocchio make a wish, and you will hear bits and pieces of the song "When You Wish Upon a Star" played throughout the show.

Epcot

The only Pinocchio reference found in Epcot is in **World Show-case**.

10) **Character Meet and Greet Alert!** If Foulfellow hasn't "Hi Diddle Dee Dee'd" you into anything, head left while facing World Showcase Lagoon to experience World Showcase in a clockwise fashion. Just after Germany and before The American Adventure, you will arrive in **Italy**, the country where the story of Pinocchio originated. While here, you may be able to meet Gideon and Foulfellow once again. However, if these two tricksters are not around, Pinocchio and Geppetto are sometimes available for meet and greets.

Fun Fact: Unlike most Disney films, Pinocchio actually has several villains. Gideon and Foulfellow convince him to skip school, join a puppet show, and visit Pleasure Island. Stromboli wants to chop Pinocchio into firewood, The Coachman turns boys like Pinocchio into donkeys, and Lampwick may have been Pinocchio's "best friend," but was a terrible influence. To top it all off, Monstro swallows Geppetto, Cleo, and Figaro and later tries to eat them. That's just as many antagonists as protagonists who consist of Pinocchio, Geppetto, Jiminy Cricket, Figaro, Cleo, and The Blue Fairy!

Disney's Hollywood Studios

After entering Disney's Hollywood Studios, walk down Hollywood Boulevard to the Sorcerer's Hat and take a right to enter the **Animation Courtyard**.

11) While your host is talking at the beginning of **The Magic of Disney Animation** show, a variety of Disney animated characters will appear briefly on the screen. Watch extremely closely to find Jiminy Cricket!

Fun Fact: Pinocchio was the first of several Disney characters who wished to be human. Others include King Louie from The Jungle Book, Ariel from The Little Mermaid, Kuzko from The Emperor's New Groove, Kenai from Brother Bear, and the Beast and his staff from Beauty and the Beast.

12) During the film **Walt Disney: One Man's Dream** you can see a quick clip of Pinocchio during the "I've Got No Strings" scene.

At the end of your day at Disney's Hollywood Studios, try to catch a performance of **Fantasmic!** Watch for four different references to Pinocchio during the show.

13) You can find Pinocchio and two of the puppets from Stromboli's show dancing in their own bubbles while an instrumental version of "I've Got No Strings" plays overhead during the "Dancing Bubbles" scene of **Fantasmic!**

14) The "Dancing Bubbles" scene of **Fantasmic!** ends with footage from the film where Jiminy Cricket is in a bubble and loses his hat. If you pay attention, you will realize Jiminy is the only character whose voice you hear through the sequence.

15) Shortly after Jiminy Cricket's appearance in **Fantasmic!** there is a semi-scary scene which involves Monstro the Whale on the water screen.

16) During the finale of **Fantasmic!** the Steamboat Willie ship sails in front of the island. As it sails by, keep your eyes peeled for Geppetto and Pinocchio who are present the majority of the time.

Fun Fact: Did you know there are no female humans in Pinocchio? The only two females, The Blue Fairy and Cleo, are a fairy and a fish.

Disney's Animal Kingdom

How does a wooden puppet fit into the animal world? Well, his father has a cat and a fish. The two villains who always steer him away from where he should be going are a fox and a cat. He almost turned into a donkey and was eventually swallowed by a whale! Oh yeah, and his conscious is a cricket.

After entering Disney's Animal Kingdom, head towards Africa and hop on the train for **Rafiki's Planet Watch** for the only reference to Pinocchio throughout the entire park.

> 17) **Character Meet and Greet Alert!** After arriving at Rafiki's Planet Watch, go to **Conservation Station** for a chance to meet everyone's favorite cricket. Jiminy Cricket is available for meet and greets the majority of the time, but make sure to check with a cast member to find out if he is present while you are visiting.

Downtown Disney

While at **Downtown Disney Marketplace**, you can find six more references to the film.

> 18) At one of the entrances to **Disney's Pin Traders**, you can find statues of Daisy and Donald. Take a close look at Daisy's lanyard to find pins of Pinocchio, Jiminy Cricket, Cleo, and Figaro!

> 19) **Once upon a Toy** is home to the largest Pinocchio in Walt Disney World. Stand by the fountain outside Earl of Sandwich and look through the round window above the entrance. To the left side of the window, there are Disney Monopoly cards including one for Pleasure Island from Pinocchio.

Fun Fact: The Pleasure Island from Pinocchio actually did not inspire Pleasure Island at Downtown Disney. Disney has a completely different back story for this Pleasure Island, which was founded by Merriweather Pleasure, a fictional character.

20) Enter **World of Disney** through "Princess Hall" and enter the second room on your left hand side. You will know you are in the correct location when you see Pinocchio standing in the middle of the room. Pleasure Island landmarks are on the ceiling and paintings of individual scenes from the film are above the wall displays.

21) Head towards the "Magic Room" in **World of Disney**, which is in the back left hand corner of the store when you enter from the Village Lake side. While in this room, look up to find several Disney characters that use magic in their respectable films including the Blue Fairy.

22) While walking around **Downtown Disney's Marketplace**, you may hear the song "When You Wish Upon a Star."

23) Just after entering **DisneyQuest**, but before boarding the elevators, take a look at the top of the pillars in the center of the room. One of the characters found here is Pinocchio.

Resorts

All-Star Movies is home to a pair of Pinocchio references.

24) You can find a poster for Pinocchio at the **World Premiere** food court located inside **All-Star Movies**.

25) While waiting for the buses at **All-Star Movies**, take a look at the windows behind you to find Jiminy Cricket and Pinocchio among several other characters.

The final reference to Pinocchio can be found in every **Walt Disney World Resort**.

26) If you are staying at any **Walt Disney World Resort**, you can find this reference within your room. The backside of your room door has some safety advice from Pinocchio and Jiminy Cricket. Also, take a look at the trash cans found within your hotel room because Jiminy Cricket is on the majority of them pointing out that he wants "you to recycle."

Fun Fact: Pinocchio goes through several transformations throughout the film. He begins as a puppet that turns into a live puppet. His nose grows, creating birds in the process, and then shrinks. He grows a donkey's tail and ears and, at the end of the film, he turns into a real boy!

"Fantasia"

Released: November 13, 1940

The Film in Three Paragraphs

Unlike Snow White and the Seven Dwarfs or Pinocchio, Fantasia does not focus around a primary story, but several stories told through music. The film begins with an introduction by narrator Deems Taylor, who later provides an introduction to each segment of the film. The first segment of the film is "Toccata And Fugue In D Minor" by Johann Sebastian Bach. The Disney animation for this part of the film consists of abstract images flowing with the music.

The second segment of the film is "The Nutcracker Suite" by Pyotr Ilyich Tchaikovsky. The segment consists of a ballet of leaves, mushrooms, fish, and various other natural elements dancing with one another. The third sequence, and probably the most famous, is "The Sorcerer's Apprentice" by Paul Dukas. The animation for this sequence follows Mickey Mouse as he borrows his master's hat and performs magic on his own. This results in a flood! The following sequence is "The Rite of Spring" by Igor Stravinsky which focuses on the creation of the world and the destruction of the dinosaurs.

After an intermission, there is a brief sequence where we meet the soundtrack of the film which is portrayed by an animated line. The next sequence is "The Pastoral Symphony" by Ludwig van Beethoven that concentrates on mythical creatures including Pegasus, Centaurs, and the Roman gods. "Dance of the Hours" by Amilcare Ponchielli is an amazing ballet sequence where the key players consist of elephants, ostriches, hippos, and alligators. The film closes with a combination of Modeste Moussorgasky's "Night On Bald Mountain" and Franz Schubert's "Ave Maria." The sequence begins with the demon Chernabog calling the souls from their graves, but in the end he is driven away by the church bells and the singing of "Ave Maria" by the townsfolk.

Note: References to Fantasia 2000 can be found in its own section later in this book.

Magic Kingdom

You can begin finding references to Fantasia on **Main Street, USA**.

1) The first reference can be found in the backroom of **Exposition Hall**. The mural on the back wall focuses on the Milestones in Disney Animation and shows Sorcerer Mickey. You can also find Sorcerer Mickey on a lightly drawn film reel that overlaps the rest of the drawings. Before leaving, be sure to read why Fantasia is considered a milestone on a plaque below the painting.

2) About a third of the way down Main Street on your right hand side is the **Main Street Cinema**. Take a look at the

films that are showing in the theatre. Under the word "Action," you can find Mickey as the Sorcerer's Apprentice.

If you love the Sorcerer's Apprentice, head on over to **Fantasyland** for some 3-D fun!

3) The Sorcerer's hat plays a major role throughout **Mickey's Philharmagic** as Donald tries to retrieve it; he even has an encounter with the brooms from The Sorcerer's Apprentice sequence.

The remaining references to Fantasia in the Magic Kingdom can be found during the **Parades** and **Wishes**.

4) The night time parade, **SpectroMagic**, provides a great variety of characters from Fantasia. There is one float dedicated to the crocodiles, hippos, and ostriches, and yes, they are all dancing.

5) The center piece for one of the floats in **SpectroMagic** is Bacchus, the Roman god of wine and intoxication, from the "The Pastoral Symphony" segment of the film. His mule may not be with him on the float, but there are dancing ostriches just below him.

6) One of the greatest floats in **SpectroMagic** is the Chernabog float. This float begins with him being Bald Mountain, but in certain parts of the parade route he actually opens his wings. Take note that his wings usually do not open in Liberty Square.

Fun Fact: Even though Mickey Mouse is the only character in the film that is referred to by name, there are several other characters found throughout the film that have names including Peter Pegasus (the black Pegasus), Yensid (the Sorcerer), Chernabog (the demon), Ben Ali Gator (the main alligator), and Hop-Low (the little mushroom).

7) The final reference found in the Magic Kingdom occurs during **Wishes**, the fireworks show. If you are watching from the Hub, which is recommended, you will have a great view of the castle turning into the Sorcerer's hat during "The Sorcerer's Apprentice" portion of the show.

Fun Fact: If Walt's original plan of having Fantasia change continuously was successful we would have a reference in Epcot during the show, Impressions De France. This show features the song "Clair de Lune" by Claude Debussy, which was originally planned to be part of a future Fantasia segment. However, the music was changed and it became "The Blue Bayou" scene in the film Make Mine Music.

Disney's Hollywood Studios

References for Fantasia begin immediately on **Hollywood Boulevard**, the main street at Disney's Hollywood Studios. Therefore, take a stroll into the movies and enjoy!

8) While in **Mickey's of Hollywood**, the first shop on your left hand side, take note that each room features a different milestone in Mickey's wonderful film history. In the room furthest from the entrance you will find Sorcerer Mickey in the center of the room. Also take a look at the area near the ceiling to find some of the brooms from "The Sorcerer's Apprentice."

9) It is hard to miss the centerpiece at the end of Hollywood Boulevard. Joining Cinderella Castle as the only symbols of a Walt Disney World park from a film, the **Sorcerer's Hat** stands 122 feet tall at the end of Hollywood Boulevard. The Earful Tower, the Mickey Mouse shaped water tower, was the park's original icon until September 28, 2001, when the Sorcerer's Hat took up residence in the park.

Behind the Sorcerer's Hat is **The Great Movie Ride**, home to three Fantasia references.

10) You will have the opportunity to watch one of the original trailers for Fantasia while waiting in line for **The Great Movie Ride**.

11) Right after the Casablanca scene in **The Great Movie Ride**, you can find Mickey Mouse as the Sorcerer's Apprentice on a screen. Interestingly enough, this room was meant to feature a tornado scene for The Wizard of Oz. Since the film already had two scenes in the attraction, Sorcerer Mickey received the privilege to be part of the ride that features some of the greatest films ever made.

12) When your ride vehicle comes to a stop at the end of **The Great Movie Ride**, various scenes from films throughout history are shown. If you have a quick eye, you may be able to spot a quick clip from the "Dance of the Hours" segment of Fantasia.

After exiting The Great Movie Ride, there is still one reference left on **Hollywood Boulevard**.

13) Near the **Brown Derby** entrance is a topiary of Sorcerer Mickey and several brooms in the grass.

Fun Fact: Did you know that Deems Taylor, the narrator of the film, is the first human to ever speak in a live action segment of a Disney film?

Head on over to the **Animation Courtyard** for references galore!

14) Just before entering **The Magic of Disney Animation**, look above the entrance to find Sorcerer Mickey.

15) You can find concept sketches of Mickey Mouse as the Sorcerer's Apprentice while waiting in line for **The Magic of Disney Animation**. If this area is roped off, ask a cast

member if you can take a look around. The majority of the time they are more than happy to let you!

16) You can find a Sorcerer Mickey statue on the left hand side of the room that features the opening show at **The Magic of Disney Animation**.

17) **Character Meet and Greet Alert!** You can meet Sorcerer Mickey in **The Magic of Disney Animation** building near the interactive game area.

18) While in **The Magic of Disney Animation,** take a look to the right of the **You're a Character** game to find two pieces of concept art for "The Pastoral Symphony" sequence.

19) A replica of the Academy Award Disney was awarded for Fantasia can be found near the exit of **The Magic of Disney Animation**.

Fun Fact: Similar to THX, movie theatres were encouraged to install a new sound system for Fantasia called Fantasound so people in the audience could have the film "surround them." Due to its high cost, very few theatres actually installed Fantasound.

20) The film in **Walt Disney: One Man's Dream** displays quick scenes from several Disney films including scenes of Sorcerer Mickey, "The Dance of the Hours," and a shot of the mighty Chernabog. Make sure to watch closely or you may miss them!

From The Animation Courtyard, make your way over to **Sunset Boulevard**, the street which is home to the famed Hollywood Tower Hotel, to find two more references.

21) Sorcerer Mickey can be found in the advertisement for Fantasmic! that is found in the windows of the connected stores **Sweet Spells** and **Villains in Vogue**.

22) Near the end of **Sunset Boulevard**, there is a sign for Fantasmic! depicting Sorcerer Mickey battling Maleficent. This billboard is at the entrance to the Hollywood Hills Amphitheatre.

The remaining references to Fantasia can be found at Disney Hollywood Studio's nighttime show **Fantasmic!**

23) There are several banners of different Disney characters on the pathway that leads to the **Fantasmic!** theatre. One of the characters shown is Sorcerer Mickey. In addition, if you look at the top of every character banner, you can find a very cool looking Sorcerer Mickey in the Fantasmic! symbol.

24) Sorcerer Mickey is one of the sections you can sit in at the theatre for **Fantasmic!** This section fills up quickly since it provides the best viewing for the show.

25) The very first scene displayed on the water screen during **Fantasmic!** is Sorcerer Mickey with "The Sorcerer's Apprentice" music playing in the background.

26) You can find ostriches, hippos, and alligators dancing in their own bubbles to the song "Dance of the Hours" during the "Dancing Bubbles" sequence of **Fantasmic!**

27) During the second half of **Fantasmic!** Mickey rubs a Magic Lamp which gives the villains power. Chernabog can then be found on the water screen as he raises the dead. He continues to appear in the remaining villain scenes of the show.

28) One of the best moments during **Fantasmic!** occurs at the very end of the show. Sorcerer Mickey appears on the top of the mountain to dazzle us with fireworks and one last magical twist to the show.

Downtown Disney

Downtown Disney has five more Fantasia references.

29) It seems that some of the brooms have escaped Sorcerer Mickey. You can find these escapees in the median between **Disney's Days of Christmas** and **The Art of Disney**.

30) If you enter **Disney's Days of Christmas** through the first door on your left hand side while coming from the Marketplace bus stop, you can find the fairies from "The Nutcracker Suite" on the ceiling.

31) If you enter **World of Disney** through the entrance below Mickey and Minnie, you can find a hat display in the middle of the room. Look at the top of the display to find a large Sorcerer's hat.

32) From the hat display at **World of Disney**, head to the last room on your left hand side. This room is the "Magic Room." You can find Sorcerer Mickey and the fairies from "The Nutcracker Suite" segment of the film on the ceiling.

33) Stop by **Planet Hollywood** on **Downtown Disney's West Side** to find Sorcerer Mickey near one of the big screen televisions in the main dining area.

Fun Fact: The sorcerer in "The Sorcerer's Apprentice" is named Yensid, which is Disney spelled backwards.

Resorts

The first resort to feature Fantasia references is the **Contemporary**.

34) Just after entering the **Contemporary** through the main entrance, you can find a statue of Leopold Stokowski shaking hands with Sorcerer Mickey. This is a recreation of the scene when the two congratulate each other during the actual film.

Fun Fact: Mickey's interaction with Leopold Stokowski was the first time Mickey ever interacted with a live human.

35) There is a topiary of Sorcerer Mickey near the **Contemporary** pool.

My all time favorite resort, **All-Star Movies**, is home to some larger than life Fantasia references.

36) After exiting the main lobby past the food court, you will find the Fantasia section of **All-Star Movies**. Sorcerer Mickey takes center stage at the pool as he stands atop rocks which spray out water. The rooms behind the pool feature brooms that are three stories tall. The center piece for the rooms on your right hand side is the Sorcerer's hat. The remaining references in this area are actually reference to Fantasia 2000. Please refer to the Fantasia 2000 chapter to learn about those references.

37) After checking out the Fantasia area of the resort, stop by the **World Premiere** food court to find a poster for the film hanging on one of the walls.

38) While waiting for the buses at **All-Star Movies**, take a look at the windows behind you. Included in the window picture are a hippo from the "Dance of the Hours" sequence and a cupid from "The Pastoral Symphony" segment. In the same window, you can find the Sorcerer's hat in the prop box!

Mini Golf

The final reference to Fantasia in Walt Disney World can be found at **Fantasia Gardens Miniature Golf Course**, near the Swan and Dolphin resorts.

39) Dancing hippos, alligators, elephants, mushrooms, Rite of Spring characters, Sorcerer Mickey, Roman gods, ostrich topiaries, the music, and even Yensid can be found at **Fantasia Gardens Miniature Golf Course**. There are two courses found here. The Fantasia Fairways is a fun, but extremely challenging course, while Fantasia Gardens has more references to the actual film. Prior to each hole on the Gardens course, there is a sign with the hole number, the title of the hole, and a poem. The titles of each hole are the actual names of the musical numbers from the original Fantasia.

"Dumbo"

Released: October 23, 1941

The Film in Three Paragraphs

Dumbo begins with a flock of storks delivering baby animals to their parents at the circus grounds. Mrs. Jumbo watches all of the other animals receive their new children, but is sadden when she does not receive her child. The following day Casey Jr., the circus train, leaves with the circus animals for the next city. While riding the train, Mr. Stork finally arrives with a baby elephant for Mrs. Jumbo.

Shortly after opening up her little bundle of joy, Mrs. Jumbo names her baby Jumbo Jr. However, after he sneezes he reveals a pair of very large ears, which cause the other elephants to nickname him Dumbo. Before performing, a boy makes fun of Dumbo's ears. An outraged Mrs. Jumbo picks the boy up and beats him. Dumbo's mother is taken away and Dumbo is left all by himself. After feeling like he does not have a friend in the world, he meets Timothy Q. Mouse.

Timothy turns Dumbo into a circus star. However, after drinking some "bad water" one night, they mysteriously wake up in a tree the following morning. After some crows suggest Dumbo flew, Timothy realizes this is exactly what happened. After much persistence from the crows, Dumbo decides to try flying and succeeds! He becomes the star of the circus and the eighth wonder of the world. In the end, Dumbo and his mother ride away on Casey Jr. in their own private car.

Magic Kingdom

Your search for Dumbo references begins before the **park entrance**.

1) Just before the **park entrance**, on the walkway between the Contemporary and the Magic Kingdom, you can find some topiaries which consist of elephants balancing on balls.

You can find two references to Dumbo on and around **Main Street, USA.**

2) In the back room of **Exposition Hall** you can find a wall that chronicles the Milestones in Disney Animation. One of the pictures shows an original poster for Dumbo which shows Dumbo flying. In addition, Mrs. Jumbo is partially hidden between Jiminy Cricket and Pinocchio's apple.

3) While at **the Hub**, located at the end of Main Street in front of the castle, you can find a bronze statue of Dumbo with Timothy Mouse sitting in his hat.

Fun Fact: Casey Jr., the train engine in the film, goes right past the future site of Walt Disney World in one of the opening scenes of the film.

Fantasyland is a place where our imaginations can be let loose, where good triumphs evil, elephants fly, and happy endings are an every day occurrence.

4) You can sit, and fly, in Dumbo while on **Dumbo the Flying Elephant**. While waiting in line, take note of the references around the attraction. For instance, Timothy Mouse stands atop the centerpiece and Mr. Stork hangs above each Dumbo's spoke. The small banners around the ride feature Dumbo and the poles which hold up these signs consist of elephants standing on top of one another.

Fun Fact: Rumor has it that Dumbo the Flying Elephant was originally going to consist of pink elephants in recognition of the "Pink Elephants on Parade" segment of the film.

The rest of the Dumbo references in the Magic Kingdom can be found during the **Parades**.

5) During the **Celebrate A Dream Come True Parade**, you can find Mr. Stork carrying Dumbo in front of Aladdin on the Aladdin float.

6) If you look closely at the snow globe portion of Peter Pan's float in the **Celebrate A Dream Come True Parade**, you will see some characters that are in a crystal like form. If you look very carefully, you will notice that one of these characters is Timothy Q. Mouse!

7) Pay close attention to the carousel float in **SpectroMagic**. One of the figures going around the float is Dumbo. If you look at the top of this same float, you will see oval shapes with characters inside. Present in one of the ovals are the crows that ask the very important question, "Have you ever seen an elephant fly?"

Fun Fact: Dumbo was supposed to be on the cover of TIME magazine in December of 1941; however, the bombing of Pearl Harbor caused these plans to be changed.

Disney's Hollywood Studios

Your first references to Dumbo in Disney's Hollywood Studios are in the **Animation Courtyard**.

8) While waiting in line for **The Magic of Disney Animation**, you can find some concept art which shows Mrs. Jumbo giving Dumbo a bath. If this section of the line is roped off, ask a cast member if you can take a look around; they are usually more than willing to oblige!

9) While your host is talking at the beginning of **The Magic of Disney Animation** show, the screen will show a variety of Disney animated characters including Dumbo!

Fun Fact: Disney used watercolor paint to save costs for the film. The next time Disney used watercolor paint in a feature film was in 2002's Lilo and Stitch.

The final reference at Disney's Hollywood Studios can be found during **Fantasmic!**

10) During the "Dancing Bubbles" scene of **Fantasmic!** you can find Dumbo, Timothy Mouse, and the Pink Elephants within bubbles on the water screens dancing to the song, "Pink Elephants on Parade."

Fun Fact: Dumbo is the first title character of a Disney film to go through the whole film without saying a single word.

Downtown Disney

11) The first reference in Downtown Disney is located at **Disney's Pin Traders**. Once inside, take a look at the pins hanging out of Donald's bag. One of the character pins here is of Dumbo.

12) The next reference is located outside of **World of Disney**.

Before you enter the store, you can find Dumbo flying with Timothy Mouse above the entrance that is near the parking lot.

13) After entering **World of Disney** through Dumbo's entrance, enter the last room on your left hand side. Included in the mural on the ceiling are the crows from the film.

14) Venture back outside and take a look into the windows of **World of Disney** that are near the Lego Imagination Center. In one of the windows, you can find Dumbo being cradled by Mrs. Jumbo's trunk with Timothy nearby.

15) While walking around **Downtown Disney's Marketplace**, you can hear "When I See an Elephant Fly," which is one of thirty-two songs played in the area.

Resorts

The only resorts that have a Dumbo reference are the **BoardWalk** and **All-Star Movies**.

16) Take a look at the tiles that surround the Luna Pool at the **BoardWalk**. It is here that you can find silhouettes of Dumbo!

17) Just after you exit **Donald's Double Features** in **All-Star Movies** heading towards the buses, take a look at the pictures in the windows. Dumbo is one of the characters present in the window on the left.

Fun Fact: Casey Jr. is named after the famous train engineer Casey Jones.

"Bambi"

Released: August 13, 1942

The Film in Three Paragraphs

The film tells the story of a deer, Bambi, also known as the Young Price, from his birth until he becomes the father of twins. The movie spotlights various parts of Bambi's life as he grows up. As a young fawn, Bambi becomes friends with other forest animals including Thumper, Flower, and Faline, a rabbit, skunk, and a young doe, respectfully. The story follows Bambi as he learns to walk and talk with his friends and the winter provides a scene of Thumper and Bambi playing on a frozen lake.

The next major portion of Bambi's life occurs the following spring when he and his mother are in the meadow. As they are eating grass, a hunter enters the meadow and shoots and kills Bambi's mother.

After the death of his mother, the story follows Bambi and his friends as they fall in love, which is called "twitterpatted" in the film. Thumper and Flower each find a mate of their own species, while Bambi and Faline fall in love. That evening, there is a forest fire. While all the main characters survive, the forest is badly burned. However, from the ashes arises new life. The following spring not only brings new plant life to the burned forest, but also twins to Faline and Bambi as a new generation of royalty is born.

Magic Kingdom

The first reference to the film can be found on **Main Street, USA.**

1) Take a look at the Milestones in Disney Animation in the backroom of **Exposition Hall** to see the lower part of Bambi's theatrical poster. To the left is a picture of Walt

Disney with one of the deer the studio brought in to understand the movements of real deer. Under the mural is a sign describing why Bambi is considered a milestone in Disney animation.

The final two references to Bambi at the Magic Kingdom can be found during the **Parades**.

2) Look carefully at Peter Pan's float during the **Celebrate A Dream Come True Parade**. Behind Peter are some characters that appear to be made out of glass in a snow globe including Thumper.

Fun Fact: Even though Bambi was the fifth Disney animated film, it began production before Snow White and the Seven Dwarfs was even released in theatres!

3) During **SpectroMagic**, look at the oval shapes on the top of the carousel float to find Bambi. A few ovals to the left of him is Flower!

Disney's Hollywood Studios

The **Animation Courtyard** has the majority of the references in the Studios.

4) While waiting in line for the **Magic of Disney Animation**, there is concept art on the walls that show what Bambi and Faline could have looked like in the film. If the area is roped off, ask a cast member if you can take a look around. They are usually more than willing to let you!

5) At the beginning of the **Magic of Disney Animation** show, pay attention to the screen behind the host to find Flower by himself and Thumper with his girlfriend.

6) You can find a sketch drawing of Thumper on the table behind the host in the **Magic of Disney Animation** show.

7) After exiting the **Magic of Disney Animation** show, look in the first office on your left to find a variety of small knick knacks from different Disney films, including a stuffed animal of Bambi that is poking out from the side of the desk.

Fun Fact: Bambi is the first Disney film to follow the "Circle of Life" theme that was also shown in The Lion King. Both films begin and end around the birth of royalty.

8) Have you ever wanted to provide the voice for a cartoon character? What about voicing Bambi, Thumper, and Flower? If so, play **"The Sound Stage"** game at the **Magic of Disney Animation** building to get your chance. After the game starts, choose the Act option and then select the Bambi scene.

9) Make sure you play **Digital Ink and Paint** while in the **Magic of Disney Animation**. This activity allows you to paint a few Disney characters including Thumper.

From the Magic of Disney Animation, go around the corner to **Walt Disney: One Man's Dream.**

10) There is a quick clip of Bambi and Thumper sliding around on the ice from the movie while you are watching the film, **Walt Disney: One Man's Dream.**

The final reference at Disney's Hollywood Studios is during the nighttime show, **Fantasmic!**

11) During the "Dancing Bubbles" sequence of **Fantasmic!** you can find Bambi, Thumper, and Flower in their own bubbles while an instrumental version of "Little April Showers" plays overhead.

Resorts

The final references to Bambi in Walt Disney World are at **All-Star Movies** and **Pop Century.**

12) There is an original poster for Bambi in the **World Premiere** food court in **All-Star Movies.**

13) While waiting for the buses at **All-Star Movies,** look at the windows behind you to find pictures of Bambi and Thumper.

14) In the lobby at **Pop Century,** make sure you check out the poster that focuses on Disney in the fifties. Flower and Thumper are on the right hand side approximately a third of the way up.

Fun Fact: Bambi's theme and format became the influence for Disney's True-Life Adventures series.

"Saludos Amigos"

Released: February 6, 1943

The Film in Three Paragraphs

The film tells the story of Disney artists and their trip to South America . It discusses the sights, music, and culture of the countries they visit. Each segment and location begins with live action footage of their visit and then the culture is communicated through animation.

The first animated sequence, "Lake Titicaca," features Donald Duck as a tourist at the famous lake sailing a boat and crossing a very unstable suspension bridge on top of a llama. The second sequence, "Pedro," focuses around a small mail plane that crosses the Andes to retrieve the mail. The journey is filled with troubles ranging from storms to running out of gas.

The third segment, "El Gaucho Goofy," provides a comparison between the American cowboy and the Argentina Gaucho. The segment is very educational with a hilarious twist by placing Goofy in situations Gauchos experience almost daily. The film's final segment, "Aquarela Do Brasil," consists of Jose Carioca attempting to teach Donald Duck the Samba.

Note: The majority of the Jose Carioca references at Walt Disney World are actually references to his role in "The Three Caballeros." Please refer to that chapter for additional Jose references. Additionally, all Donald Duck and Goofy references will be available in the next book in this series.

Downtown Disney

The first two references can be found at Walt Disney World's largest Disney store, **World of Disney** in Downtown Disney.

1) Enter **World of Disney** through the entrance below Mickey and Minnie and look just below the ceiling to find paintings of Mickey and the gang in various countries. One of the first pictures on the right shows Pedro the Airplane flying over Mexico.

2) Head into the room just below Pedro's picture in **World of Disney** to enter the "Bird Room." The ceiling mural includes Jose Carioca, who made his film debut in the movie.

Fun Fact: In the film, Pedro the "baby" airplane's wind sock consists of a diaper with clothespins holding it up.

Resorts

The last reference to the film can be found at **All-Star Movies.**

3) While waiting for the buses at **All-Star Movies,** take a look at the windows behind you to find a poster for "Saludos Amigos!"

Fun Fact: While Walt Disney was conducting research for the film in Colonia, schools were actually closed for the day in honor of Mickey Mouse and Donald Duck. Children from all around came to meet the man who created these lovable characters.

"The Three Caballeros"

Released: February 3, 1945

The Film in Three Paragraphs

The film begins with Donald Duck receiving a birthday gift from his friends in Latin America. When he opens it, he discovers three smaller presents inside. The first present is a film entitled "Aves Raras" or "Strange Birds." This movie within the movie begins by introducing Pablo, a penguin who is always cold. Pablo sets off for warmer land and eventually finds himself on his own little island. The penguin portion of the film ends with Pablo being homesick for Antarctica.

The "Strange Birds" film then goes on to look at some unusual birds from around the world. It eventually focuses on a little gauchito who goes hunting for condor birds, but instead finds a flying donkey. The gauchito catches the flying donkey and trains him to race. They win the first race they enter, but the two fly off and are never seen again. The second present Donald receives is a book about Brazil where Donald Duck finds his friend from Saludos Amigos, Jose Carioca. Jose shows Donald Duck around Baia, Brazil, where the two try to win the heart of a beautiful dancer.

After exiting the book, Donald opens his last present which contains a new friend from Mexico, Panchito! The Three Caballeros tour Mexico's culture, traditions, and locations including some popular dances, the beach, and Mexico's Christmas tradition. The film concludes with a musical recap of Donald's entire adventure. It finally ends with fireworks in each of The Three Caballeros languages: Fin, Fin, and The End.

Magic Kingdom

The first reference to The Three Caballeros in the Magic Kingdom is in **Fantasyland**.

1) While waiting in line for **Mickey's Philharmagic**, there are several posters of musicals that may someday appear in the concert hall you are about to enter. One of the posters shows The Three Caballeros with a sign which reads, "Festiva! Mariachis: !Una Fiesta Festiva!"

The only other reference to The Three Caballeros in Magic Kingdom can be found during the nighttime parade, **SpectroMagic**.

2) During **SpectroMagic**, look at the top of the carousel float for a picture of Jose and Panchito inside one of the colorful ovals.

Fun Fact: Even though Donald Duck's birthday is actually June 9, 1934, the film shows that his birthday is on Friday the 13th.

Epcot

Both references in Epcot can be found in the **World Showcase**.

3) **Character Meet and Greet Alert!** Donald Duck frequently appears in his Three Caballeros wardrobe just after the **Mexico** pavilion's pyramid. The other two caballeros rarely make appearances here anymore.

4) Inside of Mexico's pyramid is the attraction, **Gran Fiesta Tour starring The Three Caballeros**, which opened sixty-two years, two months, and three days after the film was released. While in line, you can find head shots of each individual Caballero. The ride consists of Panchito and Jose searching throughout Mexico for their good friend Donald Duck. While on the ride, be on the look out for the Donald Duck piñata, the small banners that feature the caballeros faces, and a few other fun finds!

Fun Fact: Even though the Three Caballeros' attraction is in Mexico, Panchito is the only Mexican among the three. Jose is Brazilian and Donald is American.

Downtown Disney

All of the references to The Three Caballeros in Downtown Disney can be found at **World of Disney**.

5) After entering **World of Disney** through the entrance below Mickey and Minnie, look just below the ceiling to find paintings of Mickey and the gang in various countries. One of the first pictures on the right is Pablo the Penguin in Antarctica.

6) Directly to the right of Pablo the Penguin in **World of Disney** is a picture of Mexico that features Donald, Jose, and Panchito!

7) While still in **World of Disney**, there are several references in the "Bird Room" which is located through the doors that are almost directly below the pictures of Pablo

and The Three Caballeros. On the ceiling of this room is a mural of birds that include Jose and Panchito. If you look closer, you will find the Aracuan, the bird that constantly appears throughout the film. You can also find the Arapapa bird, which is the pride of Paraguay and has the long hair, the Arapacu de Pico Curvo, the bird with the long curved beak, and the Anambepreto of Columbia and Venezuela.

Fun Fact: Although Panchito appears to be the leader of The Three Caballeros, he never appears in another Disney feature film. However, he does make appearances in some Disney comics and television shows.

Resorts

You can find quite a few references to The Three Caballeros at the shop **Panchito's Gifts & Sundries** at **Coronado Springs**.

8)   The first reference at **Panchito's Gifts and Sundries** is Panchito himself on the sign above the entrance to the store. After you enter the store, you can also find Panchito as the center piece for a fountain along with pictures from the actual film on all the walls.

9)   Just inside the entrance of **Panchito's Gifts & Sundries** is the flying donkey the little gauchito captured while hunting for condors in the film.

10) The final reference to the film within **Panchito's Gifts & Sundries** can be found near the middle of the store. Take a look up towards the right hand side near the toiletries and refrigerators to find Jose Carioca standing on a railing.

Your final references to The Three Caballeros can be found at **All-Star Music**.

11) Jose is playing his umbrella like a flute on the wall behind the concierge desk at **All-Star Music**.

12) The Three Caballeros are the centerpiece for the main pool at **All-Star Music**. The three are up to some mischief as water squirts out of Panchito's guns, Donald's flower, and Jose's umbrella.

Fun Fact: Panchito, the last of The Three Caballeros to show up in the film, does not make an appearance until forty-two minutes of the film elapses.

"Make Mine Music"

Released: April 20, 1946

The Film in Three Paragraphs

The first segment of the film, "The Martins and the Coys," features two families that live on different hills that are having a feud. After they kill almost everyone in the other family, the last member of each family, a boy and a girl, fall in love with one another. The next segment, Blue Bayou, shows life on a bayou through animated sequences and song. This segment was originally going to be a piece for Fantasia entitled, Claire de Lune. This is followed by a jazz song titled, "All the Cats Join In," and focuses around a group of teenagers running to the local soda shop to dance to their favorite songs.

The next segment, "Without You," is a ballad about lost love. "Casey at the Bat" is one of the most famous segments from the film. It is a retelling of the Mighty Casey, the local baseball hero, and his conquest to win the big game. Following Casey is a section called "Two Silhouettes." It consists of two silhouettes dancing on an animated background. Peter and the Wolf is another popular segment of the film and tells the adventures of young Peter as he goes into the forest in hopes of capturing his first wolf. "After You've Gone" is a musical segment that follows a group of instruments as they travel through an abstract world of music.

"Johnnie Fedora and Alice Bluebonnet" tells one of the greatest love stories between inanimate objects. A fedora and bluebonnet first meet in the window of a department store, are sold, and eventually try to find each other in the real world. The final segment of the film is "The Whale Who Wanted to Sing at the Met." It consists of an opera impresario who believes a whale has swallowed an opera singer and wants to save him so he can perform on stage. In reality, it is actually Willie the Whale who is the miraculous singer.

Magic Kingdom

All of the references to Make Mine Music can be found in the Magic Kingdom starting on **Main Street, USA**.

1) At the end of Main Street is **Casey's Corner**. The restaurant is named after Casey of the Mudville Mud Kings from the short "Casey at the Bat." You can find a picture of Casey and the opposing pitcher on the menu.

2) Enter the room to the right of the cashiers at **Casey's Corner** to find Mudville pennants hanging from the ceiling and a scoreboard from Republic Field. It displays the final score from the film: Visitors – 4, Mudville – 2.

Fun Fact: Sterling Holloway, the narrator for "Peter and the Wolf," may sound familiar. He has also been the voice of Winnie the Pooh, Mr. Stork in Dumbo, the adult Flower in Bambi, and Kaa in the Jungle Book.

The final reference to Make Mine Music can be found in **Fantasyland**.

3) While in line for **Mickey's Philharmagic,** you will see posters for upcoming shows at the theatre. One of the posters shown here is of Willie the Whale and reads: "I Pagliacci: performed by Willie the Whale."

Fun Fact: The Martins and the Coys, the first segment of the film, was cut from the DVD release due to the level of violence.

"Fun and Fancy Free"

Released: September 27, 1947

The Film in Three Paragraphs

The film begins with Jiminy Cricket in a house singing about how life is all about being fun and fancy free. While strolling through the house, he stumbles across a sad looking doll and teddy bear. To cheer them up, he puts in a record titled, "Bongo." The story of Bongo revolves around a circus bear who wants to live in the great outdoors.

Bongo's dream becomes a reality one day when he escapes the circus train and finds himself in the wilderness. Unfortunately, being raised in a circus, he lacks most of the required skills for living in the great outdoors. While trying (and failing) to catch a fish, he meets the most beautiful bear ever, Lulubelle, and they fall hopelessly in love with one another. Lumpjaw, a rather large, angry bear, decides he wants to be with Lulubelle as well. After a fight, and love's first slap, Bongo and Lulubelle end up together. After the record has finished playing, Jiminy is happy to see the teddy bear and doll happy again.

Jiminy then finds an invitation and decides to attend a party at the house across the way. The other attendees at the party consist of Luanna Patten, Charlie McCarthy, Mortimer Snerd, and Edgar Bergan. Edgar Bergan does a retelling of "Jack and the Beanstalk" with Mickey playing the role of Jack. Mickey, Donald, and Goofy play poor farmers in a down on its luck town, Happy Valley. After receiving magic beans in exchange for their cow, the beans grow into a giant beanstalk overnight to reveal a castle in the sky! The three heroes decide to investigate the castle and discover the stolen magical harp of Happy Valley is being held prisoner there by Willie the Giant. With some skill, and a little bit of luck, Mickey, Donald, and Goofy escape with the harp and bring happiness back to Happy Valley.

Magic Kingdom

The first references to the film are located in **Fantasyland.**

1) Contrary to popular belief, **Sir Mickey's** is fashioned after the "Mickey and the Beanstalk" segment of this film instead of the Mickey Mouse short, "The Brave Little Tailor." The outside of the store has beanstalks emerging from the roof and windows.

2) While inside **Sir Mickey's**, you can find Mickey Mouse on the beanstalk, Willie the Giant peaking in near the ceiling, and Minnie Mouse. Minnie Mouse was not in the film and is actually patterned after the short "The Brave Little Tailor." However, if you look at Mickey's clothes, you will notice it is the outfit he wore in "Fun and Fancy Free" and not "The Brave Little Tailor."

3) There is a picture of Happy Valley's castle inside **Sir Mickey's**. It is located above the door that faces towards Tinker Bell's Treasures.

4) The final reference at **Sir Mickey's** can be found outside in one of the shop's windows. In the window closest to the path to Tomorrowland, there is a poster of Willie the Giant which reads, "Giant at Large" on the wall behind Donald and his nephews.

The final reference to the film in the Magic Kingdom takes place during **SpectroMagic**.

5) During **SpectroMagic**, pay close attention to the harp behind Goofy. This is the singing harp that Willie the Giant stole from Happy Valley!

Fun Fact: Did you know this isn't the only time Jiminy Cricket and Willie the Giant appear on screen together? The two also appeared as the Ghost of Christmas Past (Jiminy Cricket) and the Ghost of Christmas Present (Willie the Giant) in 1983's "Mickey's Christmas Carol."

Disney's Hollywood Studios

The only reference to the film in the park is located in the **Animation Courtyard**.

6) While watching the film, **Walt Disney: One Man's Dream**, you will see a series of quick clips from various Disney films including one of Jiminy Cricket parachuting off a book shelf with his umbrella from "Fun and Fancy Free."

Fun Fact: At the end of "Fun and Fancy Free," Willie the Giant goes in search of Mickey Mouse through Hollywood where you can see Grauman's Chinese Theatre and the Brown Derby restaurant, both of which are represented at Disney's Hollywood Studios!

Disney's Animal Kingdom

The only reference to "Fun and Fancy Free" in Disney's Animal Kingdom can be found at **Rafiki's Planet Watch**.

7) **Character Meet and Greet Alert!** You can meet our host from the film, Jiminy Cricket, at **Rafiki's Planet Watch**.

Resorts

The final reference throughout Walt Disney World is at **All-Star Movies**.

8) While waiting for the buses at **All-Star Movies**, take a look at the windows behind you to find a film canister that is labeled, "Fun and Fancy Free."

Fun Fact: "Fun and Fancy Free" marks the last time Walt Disney would provide the voice of Mickey Mouse.

"Melody Time"

Released: May 27, 1948

The Film in Three Paragraphs

"Melody Time" is composed of seven mini musical stories. The first segment, "Once Upon a Wintertime," focuses around two couples in love, a boy and a girl and two rabbits, as they spend a day ice skating on a frozen lake. Unfortunately, the ice begins to shatter, but in the end true love prevails and saves the day. The next sequence of the film, "Bumble Boogie," is a jazzy version of "Flight of the Bumblebee" where a bumblebee flies through an abstract world.

The following segment tells the story of American Pioneer Johnny Appleseed and his journey across the country planting apple seeds and sharing hope with others. The next segment concentrates on Little Toot, a tugboat who always seems to be getting into mischief and is eventually banished from the harbor. While in exile, he finds and rescues a stuck ocean liner in a storm. By saving the day, he shows everyone he has matured. Trees, the next segment, retells the famous poem through music while taking a look at trees and nature.

Blame it on the Samba brings Donald Duck and Jose Carioca together for the final time. While sad, the Aracuan Bird from The Three Caballeros arrives and cheers them up by showing them the rhythm of the Samba. Pecos Bill is the final and most recognized part of the film. The story explains how Pecos Bill, a boy raised by coyotes, shapes Texas. Pecos Bill creates the Gulf of Mexico, makes the Rio Grande, and gives Texas its nickname, the Lone Star State. Pecos falls in love with Slue Foot Sue much to the displeasure of his horse, Widowmaker. Widowmaker bounces Sue and she continues to bounce higher and higher until she lands on the moon. With Sue gone, Pecos decides to return to his family of coyotes.

Magic Kingdom

All of the references to Melody Time in the Magic Kingdom can be found in **Frontierland**.

1) Your first reference is on the sign outside of **Pecos Bill Tall Tale Inn &Café** where you can find the hero of the final segment of the film, Pecos Bill himself.

2) Inside **Pecos Bill Tall Tale Inn &Café**, take a look above the fireplace, located on the opposite wall of the cash registers, to find a picture of Pecos Bill. Next to the picture is his hat and some rope.

3) When facing the cash registers at **Pecos Bill Tall Tale Inn &Café**, look to your right to find a map of Texas that displays Bill's travels!

4) Also in the ordering area of **Pecos Bill Tall Tale Inn &Café**, look for the picture of Widowmaker with his horse collar next to it.

5) The final reference to Melody Time in the **Pecos Bill Tall Tale Inn &Café** ordering area is Slue Foot Sue's gloves. They can be found in a glass display case with the inscription, "To Billy, All My Love, Slue Foot Sue."

6) Mosey on over to the dining area of **Pecos Bill Tall Tale Inn &Café** to find several souvenirs along the wall given by Pecos Bill's friends during their travels. Included among these items is the pot hat of Johnny Appleseed.

Fun Fact: Bobby Driscoll and Luana Patten, the boy and girl who hear the story of Pecos Bill, appear in three films together: Melody Time, Song of the South, and So Dear to My Heart.

Unless you want to grab a bite to eat, it is time to leave Pecos Bill Tall Tale Inn &Café to find the final reference in the park which is also found in **Frontierland**.

7) There are some crates just beyond the gate where the parade vehicles drive pass in **Frontierland**. If you look closely at the crates, you will notice they have, "DELIVER TO: P. BILL" written on them.

Downtown Disney

The next reference to Melody Time can be found in **World of Disney**.

8) If you enter **World of Disney** through the door that is below Mickey and Minnie, head to the first room on your right hand side. Look at the ceiling to find a mural that has

several animals in a tree including Jose Carioca and the Aracuan, both who appear in the segment "Blame it on the Samba."

Resorts

The final reference throughout Walt Disney World is located at **All-Star Movies**.

9) While waiting for the buses at **All-Star Movies**, take a look at the windows behind you to find a script for "Melody Time" in the mural!

Fun Fact: This is Donald Duck's fourth full length feature film in the 1940's. The next time he would appear in a full length feature film would be 1988's "Who Framed Roger Rabbit?"

"The Adventures of Ichabod and Mr. Toad"

Released: October 5, 1949

The Film in Three Paragraphs

The film begins with the story of Mr. J. Thaddeus Toad, Esq. from the book, "The Wind and the Willows." Mr. Toad is adventurous and freely spends his fortune on anything exciting that he encounters. Luckily for Toad, he has three true friends who look out for his best interest. They are A. MacBadger, who manages Toad's bills and financial problems, and his two sympathetic friends, Ratty and Moley. One day, after seeing a motorcar for the first time, Toad develops motor mania. Due to his spending problem, his friends lock him up in his room so he does not go out and buy a car. However, he manages to sneak out and trades his house for an already stolen car.

Toad is accused and convicted of stealing the car and is thrown in jail. After a daring escape, Toad and his friends sneak back into his house, Toad Hall, and realize he was framed. In a hectic chase, Toad and his friends attain the deed once again and clear Toad's name. Unfortunately, Toad has not learned his lesson. As this segment of the film concludes, Toad is flying an airplane and his friends realize they have a whole new problem on their hands.

The second half of the film focuses around the superstitious Ichabod Crane, a school teacher who has recently moved to Sleepy Hollow. When the beautiful Katrina arrives in town, both Mr. Crane and Brom Bones, a popular local bachelor, attempt to win her affection. While Ichabod and Katrina fall for each other, Brom Bones decides he must scare off his competition so he tells Ichabod the story of the Headless Horseman who comes out on Halloween night. That Halloween night, Ichabod has a terrible encounter with the Headless Horseman himself and Ichabod is never heard from again.

Magic Kingdom

The first references to the film can be found in **Liberty Square**.

1) After entering Liberty Square from Main Street, look at the corner of **Ye Olde Christmas Shoppe** that faces the bridge to find a sign that reads, "Music and Voice Lessons by appointment: Ichabod Crane, Instructor."

2) Just across the street from Ye Olde Christmas Shoppe is **Sleepy Hollow**, which is named after the town Ichabod Crane lived in. You can find a sign featuring the Headless Horseman attached to the front of the store.

3) **That's Debatable!** Near the **Haunted Mansion** is a weathervane of a horse on top of the building that once housed the fast pass distribution. I have discussed with

several friends and cast members on whether or not this horse would be the horse of the famed Headless Horseman. Some believe that it is since it is near the Haunted Mansion, therefore adding another layer of spookiness to the attraction. Others disagree since the Headless Horseman is not present. In addition, some argue it would be closer to Sleepy Hollow if it were the Headless Horseman's horse. I personally do not believe it is the Headless Horseman's horse. However, there are a great number of people who believe this is the horse, so I am bringing the horse to your attention. You can come to your own conclusion. Personally, I believe it is a reference to the film, "Johnny Tremaine."

4) As a lot of hardcore Walt Disney World fans and Mr. Toad fans know, there used to be an attraction called Mr. Toad's Wild Ride in Fantasyland where Winnie the Pooh now stands. Unfortunately in 1998, Mr. Toad's Wild Ride closed. In honor of the attraction and Mr. Toad, a statue of Mr. Toad was placed in the **Pet Cemetery**, which is located on your left hand side after you exit **The Haunted Mansion**. The statue of Mr. Toad can be found in the back left corner of the cemetery.

Fun Fact: Did you know that the attraction, Mr. Toad's Wild Ride, in Walt Disney World was different from the one in Disneyland? The ride in Walt Disney World provided guests the option to go on two separate tracks, which in turn provided two different ride experiences.

Your next reference can be found in **Fantasyland**, the former home of Mr. Toad's Wild Ride.

5) While on **The Many Adventures of Winnie the Pooh**, make sure you look for two references in Owl's house during the very blustery day scene. After going past Rabbit's garden, you will enter Owl's house. Look at the floor to

find a picture of Moley and Winnie the Pooh outside of Pooh's house. On the wall just above it is a picture of Mr. Toad handing the deed over to Owl. This, of course, symbolizes the fact that Mr. Toad's Wild Ride was once at this specific location. You also may recall that in the film the deciding factor on whether or not Toad was guilty or innocent came down to the deed.

Fun Fact: Mr. Toad's Wild Ride is not just honored on the attraction and in the cemetery, but backstage as well! Behind The Many Adventures of Winnie the Pooh is a break room for cast members that has pictures of Mr. Toad hanging on the walls.

One of the coolest character sightings can be found during **Mickey's Not So Scary Halloween Parade** which occurs during the event Mickey's Not So Scary Halloween Party in September and October.

6) If you are lucky enough to attend **Mickey's Not So Scary Halloween Party**, make sure you watch the parade that occurs every night. A few minutes before the actual floats arrive, you can see the Headless Horseman gallop past. He can be seen on the entire parade route, but I personally enjoy watching him from Liberty Square near Sleepy Hollow since it seems the most fitting.

Downtown Disney

The next reference to The Adventures of Ichabod and Mr. Toad can be found at **World of Disney** in Downtown Disney.

7) If you enter **World of Disney** through the doors that are below Mickey and Minnie, you will enter a room with a high ceiling. Near the ceiling on the left hand side is a picture of Mr. Toad in his red motorcar with his friends Ratty, Moley, and A. MacBadger. In front of the car, and fleeing the scene, are those pesky weasels.

Resorts

The final reference can be found at **All-Star Movies**.

8) While waiting for the buses at **All-Star Movies**, take a look at the windows behind you to find a film canister which is labeled, "Ichabod & Mr. Toad."

Fun Fact: The Adventures of Ichabod and Mr. Toad was not the only time Toad, Ratty, Moley, MacBadger, Cyril, and the weasels shared the screen together. They all appeared in 1983's Mickey's Christmas Carol as well!

"Cinderella"

Released: February 15, 1950

The Film in Three Paragraphs

After Cinderella's mother passes away, her father remarries so she can have a mother. Unfortunately, her father marries Lady Tremaine, an evil stepmother who has two daughters herself named Anastasia and Drizella. Cinderella's father dies shortly after. Years pass and Cinderella is forced to be a servant to her step family in her own house, but she remains optimistic. At the palace, the King and the Grand Duke are discussing the King's desire to be a grandfather. The King decides they will host a royal ball where all eligible maidens in the country must attend in hopes that his son, Prince Charming, will fall in love with one.

Cinderella and her step family get extremely excited when they hear the news. However, Lady Tremaine assigns extra chores to Cinderella hampering her ability to attend the ball. To help Cinderella, her animal friends make a dress for her and surprise her when she completes her chores. When Lady Tremaine sees the dress, she points out to her daughters that the materials used were theirs. In an angry rage, they tear apart her dress and leave for the ball without Cinderella.

While devastated about the ball, Cinderella's Fairy God-mother appears and makes Cinderella a coach out of a pumpkin, gives her a beautiful dress, and a wonderful pair of glass slippers. However, she warns Cinderella the spell will break at midnight. As soon as Cinderella arrives at the ball, she catches the eye of the prince. She loses track of time and flees from the ball as the clock strikes midnight. In her haste, she leaves behind one of her glass slippers. In order to find Cinderella, the Grand Duke travels the country with the glass slipper and, by order of the King, whoever the slipper fits will be the bride of the Prince. Although Lady Tremaine locks Cinderella in her room, her mice friends come to the rescue just before the Grand Duke leaves so she could show him the other glass slipper. Of course, the story ends with Cinderella and Prince Charming living happily ever after.

Magic Kingdom

Start off on **Main Street, USA** for your first group of references.

1) The most appropriate reference to start with for Cinderella is **Cinderella Castle** at the end of Main Street, USA. Not only is Cinderella Castle the symbol of the Magic King-dom, it is also the most photographed item by amateur photographers in the entire world. Since Walt and his ani-mators did not plan for the castle in the film to become a park icon, this castle does not look like the one in the film.

Fun Fact: There is a penthouse within the castle that was built for the Disney family. However, Walt never got to stay within the cas-tle or even set foot in the completed park. During the Year of a Mil-lion Dreams in 2007-2008, each day one lucky guest and his or her party was selected to stay within the castle on that particular night.

2) After seeing Cinderella Castle, visit the back room of **Exposition Hall** to see the Milestones in Disney Animation. One of the pictures that is present, but very hard to see, is Prince Charming dancing with Cinderella. The picture is just an outline and it overlaps the picture of Walt with Bambi and John from Peter Pan.

Fantasyland is your next stop for several Cinderella references! Start your tour of Fantasyland by going through the castle from Main Street, USA.

3) While traveling through **Cinderella Castle** from Main Street USA, look at the Mosaic Murals on your left hand side. The pictures actually tell the Cinderella story! A popular find in the mural is the step sisters' faces. Notice that Drizella's face is green with envy while Anastasia's is red with anger. Also pay attention to the stone work in between murals to find Cinderella's animal friends.

4) **Character Meet and Greet Alert!** Occasionally you can meet Cinderella and other characters from the film inside the waiting area for the restaurant **Cinderella's Royal Table.**

5) In the waiting area for **Cinderella's Royal Table,** look near the ceiling on the right hand side of the elevator to find Jaq and Gus high on a ledge.

6) On the climb up the steps to **Cinderella's Royal Table,** there is a very cool stained glass window of Cinderella on your left hand side.

7) **Character Meet and Greet Alert!** Every morning you can meet Cinderella, Suzy and Perla (two of the female mice), and the Fairy Godmother at **Cinderella's Royal Table**'s Once Upon a Time Character Breakfast. Please note that you need to make reservations in order to eat here.

Fun Fact: Before 1997, Cinderella's Royal Table was actually called King Stefan's Banquet Hall. King Stefan is actually the father of Princess Aurora, or as most know her, Sleeping Beauty.

8) After exiting Cinderella Castle, head directly to your left while heading into Fantasyland to find **Cinderella's Fountain**. Cinderella is in the center of the fountain with some of the mice at her feet. If you kneel down for a drink, be sure to look at how the crown painted on the wall lines up onto Cinderella's head!

9) Go around the corner towards the heart of Fantasyland to catch a ride on **Cinderella's Golden Carrousel**. As you enter the line and wait for your turn, there are a couple of interesting details to admire. First, the main sign has a few of the characters represented. Second, look at the panels near the top of the carrousel to find 18 painted panels that retell the story of Cinderella.

10) Each horse is unique on **Cinderella's Golden Carrousel** with two being extra special. The horse that is two rows in and has a golden ribbon tied to the horse's tail and purple flowers tied to the mane belongs to Cinderella. The horse to the right of Cinderella's belongs to Prince Charming!

11) While facing the castle, take the path to the left which leads not only to Tomorrowland, but also to **Cinderella's Wishing Well**. Again, take a look at the detail to find some of Cinderella's animal friends.

12) **Character Meet and Greet Alert!** Depending on the time of day and how busy the park is, you can sometimes find Lady Tremaine, Anastasia, and Drizella in the **Fairy Tale Gardens** when Belle is not putting on her show.

Fun Fact: This was not the first time Walt Disney tackled the popular Rags to Riches story. He also did a Laugh-O-Gram version of the story in 1922.

The rest of the Cinderella references found at the Magic Kingdom occur during the **Fireworks, Parades, and Shows**.

13) During the princess segment of the show **Dream Along With Mickey,** a stage show in front of the castle, you can see Cinderella and Prince Charming dancing with their other royal friends.

14) You can find Suzy and Perla, the female mice, Lady Tremaine, Anastasia, and Drizella following Peter Pan's float in the **Celebrate A Dream Come True Parade.** The float behind them carries the Fairy Godmother, Cinderella, and Prince Charming.

15) Jaq, Gus, Prince Charming, and Cinderella are all on a pumpkin carriage float during **SpectroMagic.**

16) Several characters proclaim their wishes during the night-time fireworks show, **Wishes,** including Cinderella.

Fun Fact: Prior to 1950, the Cinderella story did not include any secondary animal characters. The Disney Company created the wonderful characters of Jaq, Gus, Bruno, Lucifer, and so many more to have a secondary storyline in the film.

Epcot

The only two references to Cinderella in Epcot can be found in **World Showcase.**

17) **Character Meet and Greet Alert!** Every morning you can meet Cinderella and her princess friends at **Akershus' Princess Storybook Breakfast** located in **Norway.**

18) The only other reference is in the **France** pavilion. In the shop **Plume et Palette** is a book that is entitled, "Cendrillon."

Fun Fact: Unless you count Ichabod Crane or Pinocchio, this was the first time a human was the title character of a Disney animated film since Snow White in 1937.

Disney's Hollywood Studios

Your first references to Cinderella at Hollywood Studios can be found in **The Animation Courtyard**.

19) While waiting in line for the **Magic of Disney Animation**, you can find different pictures of concept art. One picture shows Cinderella and Prince Charming at the early stages of production and another picture shows Cinderella and Prince Charming dancing to the song, "So this is Love." If you visit on a day when this portion of the line is not being used, ask a cast member if you can take a look around. They are usually more than happy to let you.

20) After watching the **Magic of Disney Animation** show, look in the first work space on your left hand side. On the bulletin board in this room are several sketches for Cinderella. One group shows a particular frame of film from the early sketches to the final look including one that portrays the "Bibbidi-Bobbidi-Boo" scene.

21) Have you ever wondered if you and Cinderella have more in common than you thought? Find out by playing the **"You're a Character"** game in the **Magic of Disney Animation**. Please note that your results may not always be Cinderella, but if your goal is to have Cinderella as the result in the end, try to answer the questions in a way you believe Cinderella would answer them.

Fun Fact: While you are in line for the Magic of Disney Animation, head to the right before entering the theatre. At the bottom of the steps are hand prints from some of Disney's most famous animators. One of them, Marc Davis, was the supervising artist for

Cinderella. He was also in charge of Alice from Alice in Wonderland, Cruella De Vil, and everyone's favorite fairy, Tinker Bell.

22) During the film, **Walt Disney: One Man's Dream**, there are several quick scenes from Disney films including one from Cinderella.

Your next reference is present during the **Studio Backlot Tour**.

23) While riding the **Studio Backlot Tour**, you will go through a tunnel that takes you past the costuming department. The signs above the stations consist of Cinderella's animal friends that are found throughout the film. Disney must have thought they did a great job with Cinderella's dress and hired them for a full time gig.

At the end of your day at Disney's Hollywood Studios, make sure to catch **Fantasmic!** for your final two Cinderella references in the park. Please note that Fantasmic! is not offered every night.

24) During the "Dancing Bubbles" sequence of **Fantasmic!** look for Cinderella, her Fairy Godmother, Suzy, Perla, Jaq, and Gus in their own bubbles while an instrumental version of "The Work Song" plays overhead.

25) You can find Prince Charming dancing with Cinderella on the water screen during the "Princess Medley" portion of **Fantasmic!**

Fun Fact: Cinderella is the oldest of the Disney animated films to be made into a trilogy of films. Bambi and Fantasia both got sequels, but never a third film.

Downtown Disney

As soon as you arrive at **Downtown Disney's Marketplace**, make your way over to **Once Upon a Toy** for your first reference.

26) The only reference at **Once Upon a Toy** can be found in the window to the right of the back entrance. Six Disney princesses, including Cinderella, are pictured in the window.

After you have found Cinderella and her friends, go over to the **Marketplace's Guest Relations** for your next reference.

27) While in the **Marketplace's Guest Relations**, look at the portraits on the walls to find one of Cinderella. A section of this room is the Bibbidi Bobbidi Photo Boutique, which also plays host to a picture of Cinderella.

Wander on over to **World of Disney** for your next references in Downtown Disney.

28) Above the entrance to **World of Disney** that is closest to the Lego Imagination Center is Cinderella's Pumpkin Carriage. A statue of Cinderella is located to the left of this same entrance.

29) After entering **World of Disney** under Cinderella's carriage, turn around to see a sign that reads "Happily Ever After" above the exit. The sign features a picture of Cinderella with eight other princesses.

30) In the same room in **World of Disney** is a banner of Cinderella and Prince Charming together on your left hand side while facing the back of the shop.

31) There are stained glass windows with pictures of castles at the back of the same room in **World of Disney**. The castle that is second from the right belongs to Prince Charming.

32) The next stop in **World of Disney** is the "Bird Room," the room with the mural of birds on the ceiling. The mural on the ceiling contains some of the mice from the film including Suzy and some of the birds that Cinderella is friends with.

33) Your final reference in **World of Disney** is in the "Magic Room," which is located in the opposite corner of the store from the Cinderella Carriage entrance. On the ceiling are several magical Disney characters including the Fairy Godmother.

Your final reference in Downtown Disney can be found throughout **Downtown Disney's Marketplace.**

34) While walking around **Downtown Disney's Marketplace,** listen for the song, "Bibbidi Bobbidi Boo." This is one of thirty-two songs that play in the area, so the odds of hearing it within the first few songs are pretty slim. You can also hear this song inside **World of Disney.**

Resorts

Cinderella references can only be found in two resorts, the **Grand Floridian** and **All-Star Movies.**

35) **Character Meet and Greet Alert!** You can meet Suzy and Perla at **1900 Park Fare**'s character breakfast and dinner inside the **Grand Floridian.**

36) While in the lobby of **The Grand Floridian,** take a look at the floor in front of the elevator to find a picture of Cinderella and Prince Charming made out of marble.

37) Cinderella can be found in the windows outside of **Donald's Double Features** in **All-Star Movies.** The window to the left has Cinderella's glass slipper next to the prop box in the picture!

Fun Fact: The majority of the film was shot in live action format first and then transferred to animated form. This provided the animators an opportunity to gain an understanding of how the film would look with actual people.

"Alice in Wonderland"

Released: July 28, 1951

The Film in Three Paragraphs

While receiving a history lesson on the banks of a river, Alice begins to day dream about her own wonderland that consists of talking cats and rabbits who wear normal clothes. She then sees a White Rabbit with a pocket watch exclaiming he is late while he rushes into a rabbit hole. Curious Alice follows him and falls into a strange room. To get out of the room, the doorknob informs her she must drink a bottle to shrink in order to fit through the door. After she shrinks, Alice realizes that she forgot the key on top of the table and has to eat candy to grow. After she grows, she begins to cry and eventually shrinks down again, falls into the bottle, and passes through the keyhole of the door.

After wandering in a forest, Alice finds herself in a clearing where she meets Tweedledee and Tweedledum who tell her the story of the Walrus and the Carpenter. Alice quickly runs away from them at the end of their story and comes across the White Rabbit's house. She enters, but unfortunately grows once again. The White Rabbit enlists the assistance of the Dodo and Bill the Lizard to help free her from his house. Alice then eats a carrot, which shrinks her down to an even smaller size than before. At her small size, she wanders into a garden and meets a caterpillar who is no help to her whatsoever.

Alice finally meets the Cheshire Cat, who informs her where the White Rabbit went. Along the way, she meets the Mad Hatter and the March Hare at their Unbirthday Party. Craziness ensues, but the White Rabbit arrives, which leads Alice on another frantic chase after him. After losing the White Rabbit once more, Alice is lost and alone in the woods. The Cheshire Cat reappears and shows her his short cut to meet the Queen. Alice immediately displeases the Queen, forcing Alice to run away. She arrives at the doorknob again and sees herself through the keyhole asleep. Alice wakes herself up and proves that Disney does not always think a dream coming true is the ideal.

Magic Kingdom

Your adventure through this wonderland begins on **Main Street, USA.**

1) Your first stop on Main Street, USA is in the back room of **Exposition Hall.** Included in the Milestones in Disney Animation on the back wall is a picture of Alice and the Mad Hatter during the tea party scene of the film.

Your next stop isn't a Wonderland, but it sure is close. Head on over to **Fantasyland** for three more references!

2) You can hop in a teacup and live out your own mad tea party at the **Mad Tea Party.** The dormouse pops out of the center teacup and some of the characters are on the sign out front. You can also find some topiaries of your favorite characters near the attraction!

Fun Fact: Did you know there is a Mad Tea Party themed ride in each of the Magic Kingdom's around the world? Unlike Walt Disney World, Disneyland's Mad Tea Party has no covering.

3) **Character Meet and Greet Alert!** You can usually find Alice and some other characters from the movie including Tweedledee and Tweedledum, the Mad Hatter, and the Queen of Hearts around the **Mad Tea Party** area. They can usually be found throughout the day in this area.

4) The music playing in the background in **Fantasyland** near the **Mad Tea Party** is from Alice in Wonderland. This music is also playing in the Enchanted Grove area and the nearby restrooms.

Fun Fact: The Dormouse was the only character who appears in the film that was not in the original book.

The remaining Magic Kingdom references can be found during **Fireworks, Parades, and Shows**.

5) During the **Celebrate A Dream Come True Parade**, you can find Tweedledee and Tweedledum leading Peter Pan's float on the parade route. The Mad Hatter and Alice can be found on the float with Peter Pan and Wendy and with a careful eye, you can spot the Cheshire Cat on the merry-go-round portion of the same float.

6) A group of cards are painting the roses red on a float towards the end of **SpectroMagic**. Following them is Alice and the White Rabbit, while the Queen of Hearts can be found walking behind their float.

Fun Fact: The Mad Tea Party is not the only Alice in Wonderland based attraction. Disneyland has an Alice in Wonderland "dark ride" similar to "Snow White's Scary Adventures." Disneyland Paris has an Alice in Wonderland maze inspired by the one Alice finds herself in at the end of the film.

Epcot

The only Alice in Wonderland reference found within Epcot is in **World Showcase**.

7) **Character Meet and Greet Alert!** Several characters from the film can often be found in the **United Kingdom** pavilion. Alice, the Queen of Hearts, the White Rabbit, Tweedledee and Tweedledum, and the Mad Hatter are typically in the back of the pavilion by the gardens when the park is not crowded. Please keep in mind that these characters are not present at all times.

Fun Fact: The reason the "R" in March grows red during the film is because oysters were said to be best enjoyed during months that contain the letter "R." This, of course, makes the oysters in the film a little uneasy.

Disney's Hollywood Studios

The majority of the Alice in Wonderland references can be found in the **Animation Courtyard**.

8) After exiting the **Magic of Disney Animation** show, look in the first office on your left hand side to find the Cheshire Cat on a small podium and a stuffed animal Cheshire Cat hanging from a lamp.

9) Have you ever wanted to provide the voice for The Mad Hatter, Alice, or the March Hare? You can by playing **"The Sound Stage"** game in the **Magic of Disney Animation**. While there, choose the "Sing" option and select the "Unbirthday Song."

10) Is your personality similar to that of your favorite Disney animated character? It may be if your favorite character is the Queen of Hearts. She is one of the possible results of the **"You're a Character"** game in the **Magic of Disney Animation**. Please note that you may not always get the Queen of Hearts as your final result. If your goal is to end up with her, try to answer the questions as she would.

The final reference found within Disney's Hollywood Studios is during the nighttime show, **Fantasmic!**

11) During the "Dancing Bubbles" sequence of **Fantasmic!** you can find Alice, the White Rabbit, the Cheshire Cat, and the Mad Hatter all within their own bubbles while an instrumental version of "I'm Late" plays overhead.

Fun Fact: Kathryn Beaumont, the voice of Alice, and Bill Thompson, the voice of the White Rabbit and the Dodo, went on to costar in Disney's 1953 film Peter Pan as Wendy and Mr. Smee.

Downtown Disney

12) On the outside wall of **Disney's Days of Christmas**, across from The Art of Disney, are Tweedledee and Tweedledum saluting in Christmas uniforms. These two are part of Disney's version of, "The Twelve Days of Christmas." Look in and around the shop for the other eleven days.

13) There are several pins emerging from Donald Duck's luggage bag at **Disney's Pin Traders** including one of the Cheshire Cat.

Fun Fact: The film marks the first time funnyman Ed Wynn, the voice of the Mad Hatter, would work for the Disney Company. Walt would later go on to call Ed his good luck charm and would have him appear in Mary Poppins, The Absent Minded Professor, Disneyland's Golden Horseshow Revue, and many other projects.

14) After entering **World of Disney** through the doors that are below Mickey and Minnie, you will enter a long room. Near the ceiling are several pictures of Mickey and the gang on a trip around the world. When they visit Japan, they encounter the Queen of Hearts and Tweedledee and Tweedledum.

15) There is a hat display near the center of the same room in **World of Disney**. On the top of the display are some rather large hats that belong to various Disney characters including the Mad Hatter!

16) While walking around **Downtown Disney's Marketplace**, listen for the song, "In a World of My Own" from the film. This is one of thirty-two songs that play in the area, so the odds of hearing it within the first few songs are pretty slim.

Resorts

The two resorts that house references to Alice in Wonderland are the **Grand Floridian** and **All-Star Movies**.

17) **Character Meet and Greet Alert!** At times, you can meet the Mad Hatter and Alice at the **1900 Park Fare** character breakfast or dinner at the **Grand Floridian**.

18) There is an Alice in Wonderland poster adorning one of the walls in the **World Premiere** food court at **All-Star Movies**.

19) There is a picture of Alice in the outside windows of **Donald's Double Features** at **All-Star Movies!**

Fun Fact: Jimmy MacDonald, the voice of the Dormouse, was the second person to provide the voice of Mickey Mouse, after Walt Disney himself.

"Peter Pan"

Released: February 5, 1953

The Film in Three Paragraphs

Peter Pan begins at the Darling household. Michael and John, the two boys of the family, are pretending to be Peter Pan and Captain Hook which frustrates Mr. Darling who wants nothing to do with a poppycock like Peter Pan. Mrs. Darling tries to calm him down while Wendy, the teller of the Peter Pan stories, makes sure the boys are being true to the stories. After Mr. Darling gets upset with his sons and their love of Peter Pan, Mr. Darling tells Wendy that it will be her last night in the nursery. When Mr. and Mrs. Darling go out for the evening, Peter Pan arrives and wakes up Wendy and the boys and decides he will take Wendy to Neverland to become the Lost Boys mother.

Wendy is delighted and insists the boys join them. The four children and Tinker Bell fly off to Neverland. Meanwhile, in Neverland, Captain Hook obsesses over how he can catch Peter Pan and develops a plan to kidnap the Indian princess, Tiger Lily. When Peter and the children arrive, the Lost Boys, along with John and Michael, leave to capture some Indians. Instead, they are captured by the Indians who insist they have captured Tiger Lilly. Luckily, Peter sees Captain Hook taking Tiger Lily away, saves her, and brings her back to the Indian Encampment.

Hook then kidnaps Tinker Bell who, heartbroken over Wendy's arrival, tells Hook exactly where Peter's hideout is. That night, Hook kidnaps the rest of the children and leaves a bomb for Peter. The following morning, Hook convinces the Lost Boys to join his crew. However, when they find out what is to become of Peter, they opt to walk the plank instead. Peter, who has survived the bomb's explosion, comes to the rescue and saves his friends. Peter and his friends defeat the pirates and sail the pirate ship back to London just before Mr. and Mrs. Darling return home.

Magic Kingdom

Your search for references in this real life Neverland begins on **Main Street, USA**.

1) In the back room of **Exposition Hall**, the Milestones in Disney Animation are displayed on the back wall. One of the pictures shown is of Peter Pan, Tinker Bell, Wendy, John, and Michael flying.

2) Take a look at the films that are showing at the **Main Street Cinema**. Under the word "Adventure," you can find Peter Pan, Wendy, John, Michael, and Nana.

Fly on over to **Adventureland** for your next reference.

3) **Character Meet and Greet Alert!** You can meet Peter Pan and Wendy or Captain Hook and Mr. Smee at various times throughout the day near **El Pirata Y el Perico Restaurant** or the **Pirate's Bazaar**.

The next reference, which is very rare, can be found in **Liberty Square**.

4) **Character Meet and Greet Alert!** Depending on the day and on how badly Peter Pan and Wendy want to get away from Captain Hook, you can sometimes meet them on the small stage behind **Ye Olde Christmas Shoppe** near the bridge that leads to the Adventureland entrance. Please note this is a very rare occurrence.

Fun Fact: Walt Disney started working on Peter Pan during the production of Snow White and the Seven Dwarfs, almost twenty years before the film was released.

Fantasyland and Neverland pretty much go hand in hand. Therefore you are pretty much guaranteed to find a lot of references throughout this wonderful land.

5) Over the entrance of **Peter Pan's Flight** are Peter Pan, Wendy, Michael, John, and Tinker Bell flying over Big Ben and the entrance to the attraction.

6) Before heading inside of **Peter Pan's Flight**, take a look above the Fast Pass Distribution sign to find the Crocodile with the alarm clock in his mouth.

7) During **Peter Pan's Flight**, you will fly through the children's nursery, London, Neverland, and Captain Hook's ship, the Jolly Roger. You can also see all the major characters from the film including Captain Hook, Wendy, John, Michael, the Lost Boys, Tiger Lily, Smee, Nana, the Crocodile, and, of course, Peter Pan himself.

8) One of the most subtle references is found just after exiting **Peter Pan's Flight** and is to the left of the Fast Pass distribution center. Here you will find a barrel which reads, "Fire Chief: W. Ray Colburn – Lost Boys Fire Brigade." Although not a character from the story, this barrel does have a story behind it. When the original Peter Pan story was written in 1901, citizens privately contracted their own fire protection by hiring and paying a fire chief a monthly fee. If their house started on fire, that fire chief would be responsible for putting out the fire. People would put these barrels or other objects in front of their homes to show they had paid their fees. The Lost Boys chose Colburn (read it carefully) to be their fire chief on Neverland.

9) There are two weather vanes on the roof of the building that houses **Peter Pan's Flight**. One looks like Captain Hook's ship, The Jolly Roger, and the other is in the shape of everyone's favorite Crocodile. For best viewing, look towards the roof while standing near Pinocchio's Village Haus.

Fun Fact: While Peter Pan's Flight in Disneyland was an opening day attraction, Walt Disney World's Peter Pan's Flight did not open until October 3, 1971, two days after the park officially opened.

10) Donald Duck travels through several Disney animated films in **Mickey's Philharmagic**. During his journey, Donald briefly stops at Big Ben and flies over London with Peter Pan and Tinker Bell.

11) To the left of Mickey's Philharmagic is the shop **Tinker Bell's Treasures**. The feisty fairy can be found on the sign outside. While inside, ask a cast member at the register if you can wake up Tinker Bell for a very cool and secret reference.

12) As a former custodian in **Fantasyland**, the final reference in Fantasyland is very close to my heart. That's right, I'm

talking about **trash cans**! Tinker Bell is on the gold shield of every trash can in Fantasyland.

After having people look at you strangely for staring at trash cans, travel over to **Mickey's Toontown Fair** for two more references.

13) **Character Meet and Greet Alert!** You can meet Tinker Bell and her fairy friends from the Tinker Bell films at **Pixie Hollow** in the **County Bounty**.

14) There is a package from Peter Pan on the table in the front lobby of **Mickey's Country House**. On the label are special instructions which read, "USE NO HOOKS!"

Fun Fact: To help the animators visualize what the action would look like, live actors acted out the scenes on a stage. This included Tinker Bell's entrapment in the drawer where they had a live actress holding giant scissors that were about three times her size.

The remaining references in the Magic Kingdom can be found during **Fireworks, Parades, and Shows**.

15) **Dream Along With Mickey**, a stage show that takes place in front of the castle several times a day, has a portion dedicated to Peter Pan. During the show, Goofy shares his dream of having adventures while being a pirate. Peter Pan and Wendy appear while Goofy and Donald dress up as Smee and Captain Hook. They are having a blast until the real Captain Hook and Smee show up to ruin their fun.

16) During the **Celebrate A Dream Come True Parade**, you can find Captain Hook and Smee walking down the street in front of Peter Pan's float.

17) You can find Peter Pan and Wendy on a snow globe shaped float near the end of the **Celebrate A Dream Come True Parade**.

18) Peter Pan and Smee can be found walking in front of a pirate ship shaped float towards the end of **SpectroMagic**. Captain Hook is on board the ship and fires his "cannons" at the crowd.

19) One of the greatest moments during **Wishes** does not have to do with fireworks, but Tinker Bell herself. If you are in front of the castle, you will have a great view of Tink as she flies from the castle and over the bridge to Tomorrowland.

20) Shortly after Tinker Bell's flight during **Wishes**, several Disney characters proclaim their wishes including Peter Pan who wishes to never grow up.

Fun Fact: If you listen closely during the film, you will realize that both Mr. Darling and Captain Hook are voiced by the same actor. Since the original play, it has been a tradition that both characters are portrayed by the same actor.

Epcot

Peter Pan makes a rare exception in Epcot by being one of the few films that has references in both halves of the park. Your first reference can be found in **Future World**.

21) Near the end of **Soarin'**, located in **The Land** pavilion, you will soar over Disneyland in California. As you approach the front of the castle, Tinker Bell will fly in between you and the fireworks.

The only other reference found within Epcot is in **World Showcase**.

22) Towards the end of **The American Adventure** show, a video displays several famous Americans who have helped

America become what it is today. You can find Tinker Bell flying next to Walt Disney when he is shown.

Fun Fact: In 2004, Disney Publishing released the book, "Peter and the Starcatchers," a prequel to Peter Pan. The book's popularity resulted in three additional books in the series and a few short stories about what the Lost Boys do while Peter is in London.

Disney's Hollywood Studios

Peter Pan has several references in the **Animation Courtyard** area.

23) You can find concept sketches on the walls for several Disney films while in line for the **Magic of Disney Animation**. One of these drawings shows that Nana was originally going to travel to Neverland with the children. Another shows a very different looking Tinker Bell pulling the hair of an extremely angry looking Captain Hook. If you visit on a less crowded day, ask a cast member if you can take a look at the roped off area. The majority of the time they are more than willing to let you!

24) Scan the room that the actual **Magic of Disney Animation** show takes place in for your next reference. There is a Captain Hook bobble head on the same desk that has the drawing of Mushu.

25) After exiting the **Magic of Disney Animation** show, look at the bulletin board in the first office on your left. Here you can see that the artist has visited the Drawing Academy during a Tinker Bell session.

26) There is a playground styled game in the character meet and greet line on the upper level of the **Magic of Disney Animation**. The object is to mix and match body parts with different characters including Captain Hook.

27) Is your personality similar to Tinker Bell or Captain Hook? Play the **"You're a Character"** game in the **Magic of Disney Animation** building to find out! Please note that the best way to get either character as your result is by trying to answer the questions as they would.

28) While walking around the **Animation Courtyard** you may hear the songs, "Following the Leader," "A Pirate's Life," and "Never Smile at a Crocodile" from the film playing in the area.

29) While watching the film, **Walt Disney: One Man's Dream**, there are several quick scenes from various Disney films including one of Peter Pan and Captain Hook fighting. Tinker Bell can also be spotted three times throughout the show.

Fun Fact: Walt Disney's first encounter with the story of Peter Pan was during a traveling adaptation of the play in 1913.

Take a short walk, or flight, over to **Pixar Place** for your next reference.

30) While waiting in line for **Toy Story Midway Mania**, there is a giant card for the classic toy, ViewMaster. The giant card features several scenes from Peter Pan! You can see this from both the standby and fastpass lines.

The final references in the park can be found during **Fantasmic!**

31) After Mickey has finally conquered evil near the end of **Fantasmic!** Tinker Bell provides some help to make some Disney magic come to life.

Fun Fact: Walt Disney actually played the part of Peter Pan in a school play when he was younger.

Downtown Disney

The first group of references in Downtown Disney can be found in **Downtown Disney's Marketplace.**

32) They can fly! They can fly! They can fly! If you head towards the back room of **Once Upon a Toy**, you can find Peter Pan, Wendy, and Tinker Bell flying above you on the ceiling.

33) With your back to the lake, you can find a Tinker Bell topiary on the path that goes between the **Ghirardelli Soda Fountain** and **arribas bros.**

34) Before entering **World of Disney**, look at the roof to find Tinker Bell flying high as the center piece of the store.

35) The **World of Disney** entrance below Mickey and Minnie leads to a long room with a high ceiling. Just after entering the store, look up to find Wendy, John, and Michael flying above your head.

36) After finding the Darling children flying above you in **World of Disney**, make your way to the last room on your right hand side to enter the "Villains Room." The centerpiece for this room is Captain Hook's old buddy, Mr. Crocodile.

37) There are several Disney villains' hands protruding from the wall in the "Villains Room" in **World of Disney**. One of the hands, I mean hooks, belongs to Captain Hook and holds a lantern containing Tinker Bell.

38) If you leave the "Villains Room" and cross the room where you found the Darling children, you will enter the "Magic Room" in **World of Disney**. On the ceiling are various Disney characters that are related to magic including Tinker Bell.

39) While strolling through **Downtown Disney's Market-place**, listen for the song, "You Can Fly, You Can Fly, You Can Fly." This is one of thirty-two songs that is played in the area, so the odds of hearing it within the first few songs are pretty slim.

40) Tinker Bell is near one of the big screen televisions in the main dining area of **Planet Hollywood** in **Downtown Disney's West Side**.

Fun Fact: Animators studied the movements of Tinker Bell in Peter Pan to achieve the look of weightlessness of swimming in The Little Mermaid.

Resorts

Your first reference at a resort can actually be found at the **Grand Floridian**, **Polynesian**, **Contemporary**, and **Wilderness Lodge**.

41) One of the greatest hidden treasures throughout Walt Disney World is the **Electric Water Pageant**, which takes place on the Seven Seas Lagoon, the waterway between the Magic Kingdom and the TTC. During the show, an instrumental version of "Never Smile at a Crocodile" plays as a crocodile moves across the water.

42) If you are an exhausted parent, or your child loves Peter Pan, you have the opportunity to drop your child off at a supervised service for an evening called the **Neverland Club** located in the **Polynesian** resort. Of course, Peter Pan is featured on the sign above the entrance. The sections of the play area are themed around various scenes from the movie including Captain Hook's pirate ship, Skull Rock, the Darling children's room, and the clouds above London. Captain Hook, the Crocodile, and Peter Pan can also be found here.

The final references to the film can be found at **All-Star Movies**.

43) There is a poster for the film on a wall in the **World Premiere** food court.

44) After exiting **Donald's Double Features** towards the bus pickup, look at the windows outside the shop. In the upper left hand corner of one of these pictures is Tinker Bell! Peter Pan can be found in the picture on the next window over!

Fun Fact: John, the older brother, almost never made the trip to Neverland. At one point, the only people who were going to travel with Peter were Wendy and Michael due to the fact that Peter did not like that John dreamt of becoming a banker, while Michael dreamt of capturing Indians and tigers.

"Lady and the Tramp"

Released: June 16, 1955

The Film in Three Paragraphs

The film begins with Jim Dear giving Darling a Cocker Spaniel named Lady for Christmas. The three have a great life together and soon welcome a new addition to the family, a baby boy. Separately, the audience is introduced to Tramp, a dog from the streets who lives and enjoys a carefree life with no attachment to a family. His only concern is avoiding the dogcatcher.

Jim Dear and Darling leave for a trip leaving the baby and Lady in the care of Aunt Sarah. Aunt Sarah's two cats are nothing but trouble and trick Lady into chasing them through the house until they pretend to get injured. A shocked and dismayed Aunt

Sarah brings Lady to the pet store to get a muzzle. After the muzzle is put on, Lady escapes and is rescued from the dangerous streets by Tramp. The two share an intimate evening of spaghetti and a romantic walk through the park. The next morning, Tramp encourages Lady to chase chickens until a farmer begins to shoot at them. They both run away, but Lady is caught by the dogcatcher. Lady then ends their relationship. After Lady returns home, Tramp tries to apologize, but Lady refuses to accept his apology.

Just after Tramp leaves, a rat enters the baby's room. Since Lady is tied to her dog house, she can only bark. Tramp returns and saves the baby from the rat. Aunt Sarah, however, thinks Tramp was attacking the baby and calls the pound. Just as the dog catcher pulls away, Jim Dear and Darling return from their trip. Lady shows them the rat and a high speed chase is underway to stop the dog catcher from putting Tramp to sleep. With the help from Lady's friends, Jock and Trusty, they save Tramp. In the end, Tramp settles down with Lady, and the two have four puppies.

Magic Kingdom

Your walk through the park begins on **Main Street, USA**.

1) In the back room of **Exposition Hall** is a mural depicting the Milestones in Disney Animation. Included in the mural is a picture of Lady and Tramp kissing.

2) On the sign of **Tony's Town Square Restaurant** is restaurant owner Tony, who gave Lady and Tramp one of the most romantic meals any dogs, or people for that matter, have ever had.

3) While inside **Tony's Town Square Restaurant**, look at the fountain featuring Lady and the Tramp. In addition, there are pictures from the film hanging on the walls along with pictures of Lady and the Tramp painted on the window.

The window pictures can be seen from both the inside and outside.

4) Just after exiting **Tony's Town Square Restaurant**, look at the sidewalk in front of the restaurant to find the footprints that Lady and Tramp left behind in the film.

Fun Fact: Just like Main Street, USA, Lady and Tramp's hometown was inspired by Walt Disney's childhood town of Marceline, Missouri.

The final reference found in the Magic Kingdom is during **SpectroMagic**.

5) During **SpectroMagic**, pay close attention to the ovals on the top of the carousel float. In one of the ovals, there is a picture of Lady and Tramp sharing their spaghetti.

Fun Fact: The character of Tramp was actually based off a short story found in a then literary magazine, Cosmopolitan.

Disney's Hollywood Studios

The first reference in the park is on **Hollywood Boulevard**.

6) At the very end of **The Great Movie Ride** is a short film with several clips from different films. If you have a quick eye, you may be able to spot a clip from Lady and the Tramp.

After The Great Movie Ride, take a stroll over to the **Animation Courtyard**.

7) While waiting in line for the **Magic of Disney Animation**, you can find a concept sketch of Lady and Tramp enjoying dinner on one of the walls. If you visit on a less crowded

day, ask a cast member if you can take a look around. They are usually very accommodating.

8) While your host in the **Magic of Disney Animation** discusses Disney characters, watch the screen extremely closely to find Lady and Tramp together.

Fun Fact: Walt Disney actually did not think the spaghetti scene would work out very well and would not let the animators animate it. Thankfully, Frank Thomas convinced Walt it would be a great scene. In the end, the most romantic sequence in Disney history was included in the final film.

9) While watching the film, **Walt Disney: One Man's Dream**, there are quick scenes from several Disney films including one of Lady and Tramp eating their spaghetti.

After exiting the Animation Courtyard, make your way to **Sunset Boulevard** for your next reference.

10) One of the center displays in the connected villain themed shops **Sweet Spells** and **Villains In Vogue** has a very large Si, Am, and an additional Siamese Cat.

The final reference in Disney's Hollywood Studios can be found during the Studios' nighttime spectacular, **Fantasmic!**

11) You can find Peg, Lady, Tramp, and, yes, the spaghetti, during the "Dancing Bubbles" sequence of **Fantasmic!** while an instrumental version of "He's a Tramp" plays.

Fun Fact: Just after Tramp appears for the first time in the film, he walks past a barber shop. Printed on the window in very small letters is the name Joe Rinaldi, who was one of the writers of the actual film.

Downtown Disney

You can find three references to Lady and the Tramp within **Downtown Disney's Marketplace.**

12) You can find Si and Am "pins" emerging from Donald Duck's bag in **Disney's Pin Traders.**

13) If you enter **World of Disney** through the entrance below Mickey and Minnie, you will see scenes of Mickey and the gang traveling around the world near the ceiling. The scene that takes place in romantic Venice, Italy features Lady and Tramp as Tony plays an accordion!

14) While walking around **Downtown Disney's Marketplace,** you may hear the song "He's a Tramp" playing in the background. This is one of thirty-two songs which is played in the area, so the odds of hearing it within the first few songs is slim.

Fun Fact: Trusty was originally supposed to die in the film after having the horse carriage fall on top of him. Peggy Lee, the voice of Peg, Darling, Si, and Am, thought that would be too disturbing to children and successfully fought to have Trusty survive.

Resorts

Your final Lady and the Tramp references can be found at **All-Star Movies** and **Pop Century.**

15) There is a poster for Lady and the Tramp in the **World Premiere** food court within **All-Star Movies.**

16) The outside windows of **Donald's Double Features** in **All-Star Movies** contains a picture of Lady!

17) In the 1950's section of **Pop Century**, you can find two extremely large and familiar center pieces. On one side you will find Lady and on the other side Tramp, both four stories tall!

Fun Fact: If you watch the film closely, you will realize the majority of the scenes are filmed at a lower perspective as if from a dog's point of view.

"Sleeping Beauty"

Released: January 29, 1959

The Film in Three Paragraphs

After the birth of Princess Aurora, the kingdom rejoices for someday she will wed Prince Phillip and their two kingdoms will finally emerge as one. During the party, two fairies, Flora and Fauna, give Aurora the gifts of beauty and song. Before their companion, Merryweather, can give her gift, the evil Maleficent arrives. Maleficent is upset she was not invited to the party and promises that before the sun sets on Aurora's sixteenth birthday, Aurora will prick her finger on a spinning wheel and die. Merryweather then gives Aurora the gift of going into a deep sleep after pricking her finger instead of dying. Of course, the only thing to wake her would be true love's kiss.

The king orders all the spinning wheels to be burned and sends Aurora to a cabin in the forest where the three good fairies will raise her in secret until her sixteenth birthday to avoid the terrible fate. Close to sixteen years pass and Maleficent continues her search for Aurora. Meanwhile, Aurora, who is now known as Briar Rose, is celebrating her sixteenth birthday and goes out to collect berries. While out, she meets a now grown Prince Phillip and the two fall in love instantly without knowing who the other is. When Aurora returns home, the fairies tell her she can not marry Phillip since she is already arranged to marry Prince Phillip. They then proceed to take a very sad Aurora back to her home in the castle.

While waiting to meet her parents, Maleficent enters Aurora's room and hypnotizes her so she will prick her finger on a spinning wheel. Aurora instantly falls asleep causing the three good fairies to jump into action. They put the rest of the kingdom to sleep and search for Prince Phillip. Unfortunately, he has been captured by Maleficent. With the help of the fairies, Phillip escapes from Maleficent and eventually kills her. He then finds Princess Aurora in a tower, kisses her, and they live happily ever after.

Magic Kingdom

Try to stay awake as Walt Disney World is filled with Sleeping Beauty references, and they begin right away on **Main Street, USA!**

1) The first stop is the back room of **Exposition Hall**. The back wall highlights the Milestones in Disney Animation. One of the pictures shows Aurora in the forest just prior to meeting Prince Phillip. Under the picture is a description that explains why Sleeping Beauty is considered a milestone in Disney animation.

Your next stop is **Fantasyland**, the place where happily ever after occurs on a daily basis.

2) **Character Meet and Greet Alert!** If you dine during the **Once Upon a Time Character Breakfast** at **Cinderella's Royal Table,** which was named King Stefan's Banquet Hall (Stefan being Aurora's father) prior to 1997, you will have a chance to meet Princess Aurora herself.

3) After exiting the Castle, make your way to the back entrance of **Tinker Bell's Treasures**. Take a look above the entrance to find Sleeping Beauty's dress.

4) Just after entering **Tinker Bell's Treasures** through the back entrance, pay close attention to the display behind the cash register in front of you to find pictures of Flora, Fauna, and Merryweather with a dress that changes colors. Between what two colors does the dress change? Why blue and pink of course!

The next reference can be found at **Mickey's Toontown Fair**.

5) While in **Minnie's Country House**, look at the desk below the corkboard to find letters that Minnie has been exchanging with Flora, Fauna, and Merryweather.

The remaining references in the Magic Kingdom can be found during the **Fireworks** and the show, **Dream Along With Mickey**.

6) You can find Princess Aurora and Prince Phillip dancing during the stage show, **Dream Along With Mickey**, which takes place in front of Cinderella Castle. Later in the show, Maleficent shows up to ruin everyone's dreams.

7) While watching **Wishes**, you can hear Sleeping Beauty music in various portions of the show.

Fun Fact: Maleficent, in dragon form, can be found in the dungeon of Sleeping Beauty castle in Disneyland Paris.

Epcot

The first reference in Epcot can be found in **Future World**.

8) At the very end of **Soarin'** you will fly past Sleeping Beauty's castle in Disneyland.

Fun Fact: Sleeping Beauty holds the honor of being the first Disney film to have a reference in a Disney park before the film was released. Sleeping Beauty's castle debuted with Disneyland in 1955, four years before the film was released.

The two remaining references in Epcot can be found at **World Showcase**.

9) **Character Meet and Greet Alert!** The **Princess Storybook Breakfast** is hosted each morning at the **Norway** restaurant **Akershus**. Here you can meet Princess Aurora/Briar Rose/Sleeping Beauty (whichever name you prefer). This is a popular breakfast so you should make reservations far in advance to guarantee yourself a spot!

10) **Character Meet and Greet Alert!** While in **France**, you can meet Princess Aurora at various times throughout the day.

Disney's Hollywood Studios

Your first reference can be found in the **Animation Courtyard**.

11) While waiting in line for the **Magic of Disney Animation**, there is a very early concept sketch of Aurora and Prince Phillip together on one of the walls. Another picture shows Flora, Fauna, and Merryweather casting their spells upon Briar Rose to help save her from Maleficent's evil spell. If this area is roped off when you visit, ask a cast member if you can take a look around. They are usually more than willing to oblige.

Fun Fact: Just before entering the small theatre to watch the film with Mushu at the **Magic of Disney Animation**, there is a small courtyard off to the right hand side. At the bottom of the steps are the handprints of Frank Thomas, the animator in charge of the three good fairies, Flora, Fauna, and Merryweather.

After leaving The Magic of Disney Animation, go to **Sunset Boulevard** for your next group of references.

12) Inside the connected stores, **Sweet Spells** and **Villains in Vogue**, is a theme that would delight any Disney Villain fan's heart. Look around on the walls for different Disney villains including Maleficent in dragon form.

13) On the outside windows of **Sweet Spells** is Maleficent in front of the spinning wheel. A few windows down is an advertisement for Fantasmic! which shows Maleficent as the dragon.

14) You can find a picture of Maleficent as a dragon battling Mickey Mouse on a billboard advertising Fantasmic! just outside of the **Hollywood Hills Amphitheatre**.

The final references to Sleeping Beauty in Disney's Hollywood Studios can be found during the nighttime show, **Fantasmic!**

15) On the pathway leading to **Fantasmic!** are several banners of different Disney characters. On the small Fantasmic! symbol above each character is Maleficent as a dragon.

16) Maleficent is one of the possible seating sections for **Fantasmic!** The only reference to her in this section is the banner at the top of the stairs.

17) During the "Princess Medley" scene of **Fantasmic!** you can find Aurora and Prince Phillip dancing among the clouds on the water screen.

18) In the second half of **Fantasmic!** Mickey Mouse must confront villains from various Disney films. Maleficent takes center stage as she transforms both live on stage and on the water screens into an enormous dragon.

Fun Fact: Throughout the film, you can hear hints of Pytor Tchaikovsky's version of Sleeping Beauty, which inspired most of the film's music. This is the same Tchaikovsky who contributed "The Nutcracker Suite" to Fantasia.

Downtown Disney

All of the references in Downtown Disney are located in **Downtown Disney's Marketplace**.

19) On the window on the right side of the back entrance to **Once Upon a Toy** is a picture of Aurora with five of her Disney princess friends.

20) If you head over to the **Downtown Disney Marketplace's Guest Relations** building, you can find some portraits of Disney princesses upon the walls. One of these picture perfect beauties is Princess Aurora.

21) Just to the right of the **World of Disney** entrance that is closest to the Lego Imagination Center is a statue of Princess Aurora that is perfect for photo opportunities.

22) If you enter **World of Disney** through the entrance near Aurora, you can find a huge banner above the exit (inside) that reads, "Happily Ever After." On the sign are eight princesses including Aurora.

23) In the back portion of the same room in **World of Disney** are stained glass windows with pictures of castles upon them. The first castle shown on the left is Princess Aurora's.

24) The next stop is the "Villains Room" in **World of Disney**. The room has several portraits hanging on the walls including one that transforms between Cruella De Ville

and Maleficent. If you look to the left of this portrait, you can find Maleficent's hand, along with the raven, coming out of the wall.

25) On the ceiling of the "Magic Room" in **World of Disney** are several characters from various Disney films that have a connection to magic. Flora, Fauna, and Merryweather are three of the magical characters found here.

26) While walking around **Downtown Disney's Marketplace**, listen for the song, "Once Upon a Dream" from the film. This is one of thirty-two songs played in the area, so the odds of hearing it within the first few songs are pretty slim.

27) Just after entering **DisneyQuest**, but before boarding the elevators, take a look at the top of the pillars in the center of the room. One of the characters found here is Maleficent.

Fun Fact: The film, due to its length of production, cost $6 million. In its initial release, however, it only brought in $3 million which nearly bankrupted the studio.

Resorts

There are two resorts that have Sleeping Beauty references. The first one can be found at **Disney's Grand Floridian**.

28) **Character Meet and Greet Alert!** If you attend **My Disney Girl's Perfectly Princess Tea Party** at the **Grand Floridian**, you can meet Sleeping Beauty!

You can rest and find your final references at **All-Star Movies**.

29) There is a poster for Sleeping Beauty within the **World Premiere** food court in **All-Star Movies**.

30) While waiting for the buses at **All-Star Movies**, turn around and take a look at the pictures inside the windows. Flora is pictured with several other Disney characters in one of the windows. You can also find Fauna and Merryweather in the window on the left!

Fun Fact: Eyvind Earle, the background designer for the film, designed the backdrops to be reminiscent of medieval art.

"One Hundred and One Dalmatians"

Released: January 25, 1961

The Film in Three Paragraphs

The film begins with Pongo and his human, Roger, in their "bachelor pad." Pongo is determined to find his human a mate. When Pongo spies a pretty Dalmatian, Perdita, and her human, Anita, walking into the park, Pongo acts quickly and causes the two humans to meet. Both couples, humans and Dalmatians, soon marry.

Happiness is in the air as Pongo and Perdita are expecting puppies. Instead of a much larger, happy family, Anita's old college roommate, Cruella De Ville, has other plans for the puppies. Fifteen puppies are soon born and Cruella stops by and offers to buy all fifteen as soon as they get their spots. Roger turns down the offer and Cruella is furious. A few weeks later while walking in the park with their humans, two henchmen, Horace and Jasper, break into the house and steal all fifteen puppies. Pongo and Perdita use the twilight bark system (a gossip line for dogs) to put out the alert that their puppies are missing. They soon get word that the puppies are far in the countryside at the old De Ville mansion. They set off at once to retrieve their puppies.

In the meantime, Cruella has purchased another eighty-four puppies to make half a dozen fur coats. Pongo and Perdita come to the rescue and escape with all ninety-nine puppies. Hot on their trail is Cruella, Horace, and Jasper, but all the Dalmatians make it home without being caught. Roger and Anita are in shock to find they now have 101 Dalmatians in their presence, but decide to keep them all on their own "Dalmatian Plantation."

Magic Kingdom

The first reference in Walt Disney World that relates to One Hundred and One Dalmatians is found on **Main Street, USA**.

1) If you go to the back room of **Exposition Hall**, you will find a place where you can put yourself into a scene from various Disney films. One of the scenes is from One Hundred and One Dalmatians. You can go inside the television and have Pongo, Perdita, and all fifteen of their puppies watching you while Cruella De Ville, Horace, and Jasper stand in the background.

2) On the back wall in the same room of **Exposition Hall** is a picture of a very startled looking Pongo within the Milestones in Disney Animation mural.

The only other reference pertaining to One Hundred and One Dalmatians in the Magic Kingdom can be found during the **Celebrate A Dream Come True Parade**.

3) Near the end of the **Celebrate A Dream Come True Parade**, pay close attention to Peter Pan's float. Behind Peter is a merry-go-round in a bubble. Included among the characters that are circling around are two of the Dalmatian puppies.

Fun Fact: If you want to tell a boy dog apart from a girl dog in the 101 Dalmatians, simply look at their collar! All of the females wear blue, while the males wear red!

Disney's Hollywood Studios

The first reference in the park can be found on **Hollywood Boulevard**.

4) Stop by **L.A. Cinema Storage**, which is the last store on the right hand side of Hollywood Boulevard. While inside, you can find Dalmatian puppies watching the famous "Thunderbolt" on a television. To find this, look at the corner near the ceiling that faces the Sorcerer's Hat.

Fun Fact: Dalmatian puppies were in high demand after the initial release of the film.

The next reference can be found in the **Animation Courtyard**.

5) While waiting in line for the **Magic of Disney Animation**, you can find concept sketches on the walls for various Disney films. One sketch has a very similar look to the film's final appearance, although it is very difficult to judge exactly which scene is shown. If you visit on a day where the lines are not very long, ask a cast member if you can take a look at the sketches. The majority of the time they are more than happy to help you out!

Fun Fact: During the Twilight Bark scene of the film, you can see Jock, Peg, Bull, and Lady from Lady and the Tramp.

Your next reference can be found on **Sunset Boulevard**.

6) Stop by the connected stores **Sweet Spells** and **Villains in Vogue** to find pictures of different Disney villains on the walls including Cruella De Ville.

At the end of your day at Disney's Hollywood Studios, make sure you watch **Fantasmic!** for your final reference in the park.

7) Just after the Queen from Snow White transforms into the Hag in **Fantasmic!** she calls upon all the forces of evil. In response to her call, Cruella De Ville appears on the water screen and is present through the rest of the villains' sequence.

Fun Fact: The opening sequence of One Hundred and One Dalmatians was the most expensive opening up to that point for the Disney Animation Studio.

Downtown Disney

All of your references in Downtown Disney can be found in **Downtown Disney's Marketplace**.

8) There is a large statue of Patch the puppy in the shop **Pooh Corner**. Patch is here since this shop used to be connected to the shop Disney Tails, a shop for pets.

9) After entering **World of Disney** through the entrance below Mickey and Minnie, look at the painted panels near the ceiling. One of the panels on your right hand side shows Mickey and the gang at the Mann's Chinese Theatre in L.A. along with Cruella De Ville, Pongo, Perdita, and some puppies.

10) If you continue to the back of the same room in **World of Disney**, you will find the "Villains Room" on your right. There are several portraits of different villains on the wall including one that changes between Cruella De Ville and Maleficent depending on where you are standing. If you look to the right of this portrait, you can find Cruella's hand emerging from the wall with her signature cigarette.

11) While strolling around **Downtown Disney's Marketplace**, listen for the song, "Cruella De Ville" as it is one of thirty-two songs that is played in the area.

Fun Fact: The author of the novel <u>One Hundred and One Dalmatians</u>, Dodie Smith, actually had her Dalmatian give birth to fifteen puppies. Just like the movie, one of the Dalmatians unfortunately did not make it, but her husband wrapped the puppy in a towel and rubbed it back to life, much like Roger does in the film.

Resorts

The final references to One Hundred and One Dalmatians can be found at **All-Star Movies** resort.

12) If you are staying at **All-Star Movies,** you are in for quite the treat (and I don't mean a Kanine Krunchy). The resort is divided into five different films, one of which is One Hundred and One Dalmatians. The huge center piece for this area is Pongo on one side and Perdita on the other. While walking around, take a look at the ground to find several Kanine Krunchy dog bones. On the buildings, you will find 98 puppies running on the film strips. The giant Pongo and Perdita give you a total of 100. Where is number 101 you may ask? Just like in the movie, you can find Lucky watching a large television in the middle of the area.

13) Just after you exit **Donald's Double Features** in **All-Star Movies** towards the buses, take a look at the pictures in the windows to find a picture of two Dalmatian puppies from the film!

Fun Fact: Not all of the puppies have names, but here are some helpful hints to locate the puppies that do. Rolly is chubby and is always talking about food, Patch has a giant patch around his eye, Lucky's spots on his back form a horseshoe, Penny has the fewest number of spots of all the puppies, and Freckles' spots on his face are similar to freckles.

"The Sword in the Stone"

Released: December 25, 1963

The Film in Three Paragraphs

The film begins by explaining that the king has died and has no heir to the throne. To determine the rightful king, a sword is placed into an anvil upon a stone. Only the rightful King of England will have the ability to remove the sword. Years pass and still no one has been able to pull the sword from the stone. Meanwhile, a young boy named Arthur meets a magician named Merlin who decides to take young Arthur or Wart, as people call him, under his wing and tutor the young lad.

Merlin and Wart's foster family do not get along, but Merlin continues with the lessons by transforming Wart into a fish, a squirrel, and a bird to teach him that in the animal world you have to use your brain over your brawn. While the lessons continue, Wart is appointed the squire for his foster brother, Kay. Kay is entering a contest on New Year's that will determine the new King since the sword remains in the stone. Wart is very excited, but because of Merlin's magic, he is demoted from his job as squire and it is given to someone else.

Just before Kay leaves for the tournament, his new squire becomes sick allowing Wart to reclaim his job as squire. Merlin, upset by the news, leaves for Bermuda. Wart performs his squire duties at the tournament, but realizes he left Kay's sword at the Inn. He returns to the Inn, but no one is there to let him in so he decides to grab a sword that is in a nearby stone. He succeeds in pulling the sword out of the stone and returns to the tournament where everyone is in shock that the sword has been removed. They place the sword back in the stone and several others try to remove it again with no success. Arthur pulls it out with ease once more proving he is the rightful King.

Magic Kingdom

Your walk to royalty begins on **Main Street, USA**.

1) Visit the backroom of **Exposition Hall** and take a look at the Milestones in Disney Animation on the back wall. One of the pictures shown is Arthur pulling the sword from the stone.

Fantasyland is themed around a medieval fair so it is the perfect setting for your next reference!

2) Just after walking through the castle, you can find the actual **Sword in the Stone** in front of Cinderella's Golden Carrousel. Feel free to give it a tug to see if you are the heir to the throne.

Fun Fact: Although it appears to be retired for the time being, there was a show focused around the Sword in the Stone depending on the time of year. Merlin presided in the search to find the Temporary Ruler of the Realm who would be the ruler for a very small portion of the day.

Disney's Hollywood Studios

Your first reference in Disney's Hollywood Studios can be found in the **Animation Courtyard**.

3) There are several concept sketches on the walls for different Disney films in the line for the **Magic of Disney Animation**. Included in this collection is a sketch of Arthur pulling the sword from the stone. If you visit on a less crowded day, ask a cast member if you can take a look around. They are more than willing to help out!

At the end of your day at Disney's Hollywood Studios, make sure to check out **Fantasmic!** for your final reference.

4) If it was not for the sword in the stone, Mickey Mouse may still be stuck in his nightmare in **Fantasmic!** During a pivotal moment of the show, Mickey becomes the only Disney character, other than Arthur, to pull the sword from the stone.

Fun Fact: Bill Peet actually wrote a screenplay for Sword in the Stone, which was practically unheard of for an animated film at the time. Previously, animated films were all put on storyboards, which consisted of pictures that allowed the artist to see what would happen in each scene.

Downtown Disney

All of your references in Downtown Disney can be found in the store **World of Disney**.

5) Enter **World of Disney** through the entrance below Mickey and Minnie and go into the first room on the right. The ceiling is a giant mural that includes Merlin's pet owl, Archimedes. Carefully search the ceiling to locate the only boy present. Of course the boy is not a boy in the picture, but in fact a squirrel. That's right, you can find young Arthur, in squirrel form, near Zazu.

6) While still in **World of Disney**, return to the room you first entered and make your way to the last room on your left. This room is the "Magic Room." The ceiling is comprised of various characters that have an association with magic including Merlin.

Resorts

The final reference for The Sword in the Stone can be found at **All-Star Movies**.

7) Just after exiting **Donald's Double Features** towards the buses at **All-Star Movies,** look at the picture in the window to find several Disney characters including Merlin!

Fun Fact: The animators thought of Merlin as a version of Walt Disney himself. If you look closely, you will see that Merlin and Walt's nose are almost identical!

"The Jungle Book"

Released: October 18, 1967

The Film in Three Paragraphs

The film begins when Bagheera the panther stumbles across Mowgli, a man cub (a human child). He brings Mowgli to a pack of wolves to raise him as their own. A few years later, the evil tiger, Shere Khan, returns to the jungle and swears he will kill Mowgli. The wolf pack decides that Bagheera must bring Mowgli to the nearest man village to keep him safe.

Mowgli and Bagheera encounter several animals on their journey to the man village. Mowgli first meets a python named Kaa who tries to eat him, followed by a herd of elephants that are run in military style, and then a care free bear named Baloo. Baloo shows Mowgli the care free life he lives in the jungle and promises Mowgli that the two of them can stay together forever. This quickly changes when a group of monkeys kidnap Mowgli. They take him to their leader, King Louie, who demands Mowgli tells him the secret of man's red fire. A pursuit occurs and eventually Baloo, with the help of Bagheera, get Mowgli back from the monkeys.

The following day, Baloo tells Mowgli he must go to the man village. This upsets Mowgli who, in turn, runs away. He meets four vultures who declare their friendship to Mowgli, but soon the five friends encounter Shere Khan. Khan informs Mowgli he will give him ten seconds to run away, but Mowgli is not scared. Just before Shere Khan attacks, Baloo rescues Mowgli, but appears to be killed in the process. Near the end of Bagheera's moving eulogy, Baloo returns to life. Baloo again promises Mowgli that they can stay together forever. However, a girl from the nearby man village catches Mowgli's eye and he follows her into the man village. Baloo and Bagheera then return to the heart of the jungle without their man cub friend.

Magic Kingdom

Your "Bare Necessities" vacation begins on **Main Street, USA**.

1) **Character Meet and Greet Alert!** At various times throughout the day, you can meet King Louie and Baloo in front of the **Main Street Train Station** entrance. If they are not there, they might be at the **Town Square** instead. Please note that these two are not present all the time.

2) In the back room of **Exposition Hall** is a wall that showcases the Milestones in Disney Animation. One of the pictures shown is of the original Jungle Book movie poster.

The remaining reference in the Magic Kingdom can be found during **SpectroMagic**.

3) Pay close attention to the carousel float in **SpectroMagic**. One of the small ovals near the top of the float shows King Louie sitting on his throne.

Fun Fact: The original voice of Mowgli, David Bailey, had to stop because he hit puberty too early. The director's son, Bruce Reitherman, took over the role as Mowgli. If he sounds familiar, that is because he also provided the voice of Christopher Robin.

Disney's Hollywood Studios

The first reference to the film found in the park is located at the end of **Hollywood Boulevard**.

4) Since The Jungle Book premiered at the Grauman's Chinese Theatre in California, there is a reference to the film at the entrance of **The Great Movie Ride**, which is housed in a replica of the Grauman's Chinese Theatre. Before entering the courtyard, look at the windows on the left hand side to find pictures, passes, and programs from the premiere of The Jungle Book at Grauman's Chinese Theatre!

Walk to the **Backlot** area to find your next clue.

5) While waiting to board the trams in the **Studio Backlot Tour**, take a look at the props on the left hand side of the line to find a book entitled, "The Jungle Book."

The next group of references can be found in the **Animation Courtyard**.

6) While your host discusses Disney characters at the start of the **Magic of Disney Animation** show, Baloo appears quickly among several other characters on the screen.

7) A little later in the **Magic of Disney Animation** show, your host will discuss how animators bring character movements to life. During this part of the presentation, a clip of Baloo and Mowgli having a bare necessity type day is shown on the screen.

8) Have you ever wanted to be the voice of Baloo and Mowgli? You can in the **Magic of Disney Animation** building! While in the interactive area, play the game, **"The Sound Stage,"** and choose the "Sing" option to add your voice to the song, "Bare Necessities."

9) While still in the interactive area of the **Magic of Disney Animation**, try out the **"Digital Ink and Paint"** game. This game allows you to paint some of your favorite Disney animated characters including Baloo!

At the end of your day at the Studios, make sure to watch the night-time show **Fantasmic!** for your final references in the park.

10) You can find Mowgli, Louie, and Baloo all dancing in their own bubbles while an instrumental version of "I Wanna Be Like You" plays overhead during the "Dancing Bubbles" sequence of **Fantasmic!**

11) You can find Baloo on the steamboat with Mickey at the very end of **Fantasmic!**

Fun Fact: Due to the fact that this was the final animated film by Walt Disney, the price of the movie's original theatrical poster is quite expensive. You can usually purchase it at Sid Cahuenga's One-Of-A-Kind shop located in the wooden building on your left hand side just after entering the park.

Disney's Animal Kingdom

If you make your way over to **Africa**, you can find one of my favorite references throughout Walt Disney World.

12) **Character Meet and Greet Alert!** Just after entering **Africa** by crossing the bridge from Discovery Island, there is path on your right hand side that leads to Asia. There is an archway on your left hand side after taking a few steps along the path. Baloo and King Louie make appearances at various times throughout the day in front of this archway.

13) **That's Debatable!** In **Africa**, pass under the archway mentioned in the previous clue and look under the sheet that is hanging down on the wall directly to your left to

find a Baloo silhouette in the stone work. Some people I have talked with do not believe this to be a real reference to Baloo. However, I truly believe the Imagineers put everything at Walt Disney World in for a specific purpose, including the stone work. I personally believe it is a reference. What do you think?

Your next reference can be found in **Asia**.

14) Walt Disney World is filled with objects that have been individualized. The rafts at **Kali River Rapids** are no exception. If you look at the names of the rafts, which are printed on the bumpers, you can find that one is called, Baloo Me Away.

The final reference in Disney's Animal Kingdom is during **Mickey's Jammin' Jungle**.

15) It is no secret that King Louie and Baloo love a swinging beat. **Mickey's Jammin' Jungle Parade** sure does give them something to groove to during the daily parade. The two characters can be found walking in between floats.

Fun Fact: Here are some interesting Elephant Tales. The Colonel, leader of the elephants, was voiced by J. Pat O'Malley. He also provided the voice of the Colonel, a sheepdog, in 101 Dalmatians. The Colonel's wife in the film, Winifred the Elephant, was voiced by Verna Felton. She also voiced the leader of the elephants in Dumbo. Unfortunately, this was Verna Felton's last film as she passed away just hours before Walt Disney.

Downtown Disney

Your first two references in Downtown Disney can be found in the store, **World of Disney**.

16) If you enter **World of Disney** through the entrance below Mickey and Minnie, you will enter a room that shows an interesting story on painted tiles near the ceiling. Mickey and the gang are taking a trip around the world that includes a jungle scene where Mowgli, King Louie, Baloo, and Bagheera are present.

17) The next reference is in the "Bird Room" in **World of Disney**. This is the first room on your right hand side after you had entered the store. The ceiling contains several Disney characters within a tree including Buzzy, Ziggy, Dizzy, and Flaps, the four vultures that befriend Mowgli at the end of the film.

The final reference in Downtown Disney can be found throughout **Downtown Disney's Marketplace**.

18) While walking through **Downtown Disney's Marketplace**, listen for the song, "Bare Necessities" which plays in the background from time to time. This is one of thirty-two songs played in the area, so the odds of hearing it within the first few songs is pretty slim.

Fun Fact: Terry Gilkyson wrote several songs for the film, but Walt felt they were too dark. The only song he wrote that actually made it into the film was "Bare Necessities."

Resorts

Your final Jungle Book references are at **All-Star Movies** and **Pop Century**.

19) While waiting for the buses at **All-Star Movies**, look into the windows of the shop, **Donald's Double Features**, to find several Disney characters including Baloo!

20) There are two amazing center pieces in the 1960's section of **Pop Century**. On one side is a four story Baloo and on the other side is Mowgli.

Fun Fact: The Jungle Book went on to inspire a sequel and two television shows, Jungle Cubs and, my personal favorite, TaleSpin.

"Aristocats"

Released: December 24, 1970

The Film in Three Paragraphs

The film begins with Madame Adelaide, an older woman living in Paris, making out her will with her lawyer. She decides to give her entire fortune to her four cats, Duchess, and her kittens Marie, Berlioz, and Toulouse. Edgar, her butler, eavesdrops on the conversation through a pipe and is outraged to learn that the cats will come before him in the will.

Edgar quickly forms a plan to get rid of the cats. He puts sleeping pills in their cream and, after they have fallen asleep, drives them out into the country. Unfortunately for him, two dogs, Napoleon and Lafayette, attack him causing the basket holding the cats to fall out of the motorcycle. The cats are all alone in the country until the following morning when they meet an alley cat, Thomas O'Malley. Thomas quickly woos Duchess and decides to help them return to Paris.

When the cats arrive at Madame's door in Paris, Edgar hears them first and puts them into a bag with the intent of shipping them off to Timbuktu. Luckily for the cats, Roquefort, a friendly mouse that lives in Madame's house, witnesses the entire incident and warns Thomas O'Malley. O'Malley directs Roquefort to gather his alley cat friends. A huge showdown occurs in the barn where Roquefort must unlock the trunk holding the cats. After Duchess and her kittens are free, the cats trap Edgar in the trunk and he is shipped off to Timbuktu instead. In the end, Madame adopts Thomas O'Malley and makes her house a home for the stray cats of Paris.

Magic Kingdom

Your sole reference within the Magic Kingdom can be found on **Main Street, USA**.

1) Make your way to **Exposition Hall**. Once inside, head to the back room and take a look at the Milestones in Disney Animation on the back wall to find a picture of Duchess.

Epcot

Just like the Magic Kingdom, Epcot only has one reference to the film and that can be found within **World Showcase**.

2) **Character Meet and Greet Alert!** While in France, keep your eyes open for Marie. She is rarely present, but a great find when you can see her!

Fun Fact: This was Phil Harris' second time providing a voice for a character in a Disney film. He first performed as Baloo in "The Jungle Book" and would also voice Little John in "Robin Hood."

Downtown Disney

Your final Aristocats reference can be found in the store, **World of Disney**.

3) While in **World of Disney**, pay close attention to the soundtrack playing overhead. "Everybody Wants to be a Cat" is one of the songs that is played throughout the store from time to time.

Fun Fact: Thomas O'Malley's full name is Abraham de Lacy Giuseppe Casey Thomas O'Malley.

"Robin Hood"

Released: November 8, 1973

The Film in Three Paragraphs

King Richard leaves for the Crusades and his greedy brother, Prince John, takes temporary control of the country. Prince John raises the taxes so the majority of everyone's income goes directly to him. Luckily, the town of Nottingham has a hero, Robin Hood, and his sidekick, Little John. They steal from the rich and give to the poor so the poor can survive. Prince John travels to Nottingham in hopes of capturing Robin Hood. He organizes an archery contest where the winner will receive a kiss from Maid Marion, Robin Hood's childhood sweetheart.

Robin competes in the tournament in disguise and wins with ease. However, the disguise does not fool Prince John who orders Robin to be hung immediately. Robin escapes and proposes to Maid Marion. The joyous celebration and wedding are delayed as Robin must remain in hiding and the brutality of Prince John's rule intensifies. Prince John raises taxes to a level most are unable to afford. This leads to the majority of the town being sent to jail including Friar Tuck, a respectable member of the community. Prince John declares he will hang Friar Tuck with the hope that Robin Hood will no longer remain in hiding and attempt to free him.

The night before the hanging, Robin and Little John break into the jail and free all of the prisoners. As the citizens escape, Robin sneaks into Prince John's bedroom and steals all of the money back. Unfortunately, a toddler is left behind while everyone is escaping and Robin returns to save the little girl. He saves her, but in the process is trapped in a tower. The Sheriff of Nottingham seizes the opportunity and sets the tower on fire. Robin is forced to jump to the moat below and thankfully survives. Shortly after these events, King Richard returns from the Crusades, pardons Robin Hood, and orders his brother and henchmen to work in the Royal Rock Pile. And, of course, Robin Hood and Maid Marion marry at the end and live happily ever after.

Magic Kingdom

The first references to Robin Hood can be found at **Main Street, USA**.

1) **Character Meet and Greet Alert!** At times, usually earlier in the day, you can meet Prince John, The Sheriff of Nottingham, Robin Hood, and Little John in front of the **Main Street Railroad Station** or at **Town Square** around the flag pole.

2) Stop in the back room of **Exposition Hall** to find a picture of Robin Hood stealing money right under Prince John's nose on the Milestones in Disney Animation mural.

Fun Fact: After Little John breaks into the prison during the film, you can find some writing on the wall next to the door which reads, "God Forgive Prince John."

Disney's Hollywood Studios

Your final reference to Robin Hood throughout all of Walt Disney World can be found during Disney's Hollywood Studios night time show, **Fantasmic!**

3) At the very end of **Fantasmic!** you can find several Disney characters from various films on the steamboat with Mickey Mouse. Robin Hood is present the majority of the time, but is not guaranteed to be there every show.

Fun Fact: Much like Kaa in The Jungle Book, Sir Hiss, Prince John's right hand snake, can hypnotize anyone by having them look into his eyes. This would occur one more time in Aladdin when Jafar uses his staff that is shaped like a snake to hypnotize people.

"The Many Adventures of Winnie the Pooh"

Released: March 11, 1977

The Film in Three Paragraphs

The film is composed of three individual stories. The first one revolves around Winnie the Pooh and his search for honey. He begins by following a bee into a honey tree and decides to disguise himself as a little black rain cloud. He rolls in the mud, grabs a balloon, and takes flight. He does retrieve some honey, but makes the bees angry in the process. Therefore, Pooh goes to Rabbit's house and eats all of his honey. When Pooh attempts to leave through the door, he gets stuck. Christopher Robin decides the only thing to do is to wait for Pooh to get thin again. They wait and wait and eventually Pooh pops out.

The next story begins on a very windy, blustery day that Gopher calls "Windsday." Pooh decides to wish everyone a happy Windsday, but when he comes across Piglet, the two of them are blown over to Owl's house. While visiting Owl, the tree that his house resides in blows down and Eeyore assumes the responsibility of finding Owl a new home. Tigger visits Pooh that night and informs him to watch out for Heffalumps and Woozles. As Pooh dreams of these honey stealing monsters, it rains and rains and he wakes up in a flooded house. Piglet, also stuck in a flooded house, floats away on a chair until he encounters Pooh. Christopher Robin declares that Pooh saved Piglet and throws him a heroes party. During the party, Eeyore shows everyone Piglet's house and states that it is Owl's new home. Piglet gives it to Owl making him a hero as well.

The final story of the film revolves around Tigger. Rabbit wants Tigger to stop bouncing so he takes him into the woods with the intention of losing him. Instead Rabbit becomes lost and Tigger rescues him. Winter eventually arrives and Tigger takes Roo bouncing until they become stuck in a tree. While stuck in the tree, Tigger states that he will never bounce again as long as he can get down. The Narrator of the story comes to the rescue and tips the book over so Tigger can slide down on the words. Once on the ground, everyone, including Rabbit, realize they loved the old bouncy Tigger more and allow him to bounce once again. The film closes with Christopher Robin leaving for school, but before he leaves, he makes a promise to Pooh that the two will be friends forever.

Magic Kingdom

You can find three Winnie the Pooh references on **Main Street, USA**.

1) While inside **Exposition Hall,** head to the back room to find the Milestones in Disney Animation. One of the pictures shows Pooh floating from the balloon from the Winnie the Pooh and the Honey Tree sequence.

2) The next clue on Main Street, USA can be found at the end of Main Street just prior to the hub. When you reach Casey's Corner, the last building on your left hand side, take a left and go to the **Crystal Palace**. This is one of the

best places to find Winnie the Pooh and his friends from the Hundred Acre Woods. Here you can find Pooh Bear, Eeyore, Piglet, and everyone's favorite bouncer as topiaries just after entering the building.

3) **Character Meet and Greet Alert!** The **Crystal Palace** has one of the greatest character meals throughout the Walt Disney World Resort. During every meal, you can meet Pooh, Eeyore, Tigger, and Piglet as they walk around and interact with you while you dine. This is a very popular dining experience so make sure you make your reservations far in advance.

Winnie the Pooh is beginning to take over **Fantasyland**. You could not find that Silly ol' Bear fifteen years ago in Fantasyland, but he is slowly making this area Poohland!

4) While riding **The Many Adventures of Winnie the Pooh**, you will bounce with Tigger, witness the windy, blustery day (and see pictures of Owl and Pooh with past residents of the attraction's location), see Heffalumps and Woozles, and, of course, attend a hero party for Pooh and Piglet! All of the main characters from the film can be found on the attraction.

Fun Fact: The Magic Kingdom was the first Disney Park worldwide to receive an attraction based on the Winnie the Pooh stories in June of 1999.

5) After you exit The Many Adventures of Winnie the Pooh, you will enter the store, **Pooh's Thotful Shop**. Throughout the store you will find pages from the Winnie the Pooh book, which can also be found in the attraction's line and ride. In addition, the store has Tigger, Piglet, and the rest of your Hundred Acre Friends on top of the shelves. Finally, the front entrance features Winnie the Pooh himself.

6) Just across the way from Pooh's Thotful Shop and The Many Adventures of Winnie the Pooh is **Pooh's Playful Spot**. Although this spot is intended for younger children (ages 2-5), feel free to explore this miniature Hundred Acre Woods. While looking around, you can find Roo on the front sign welcoming you to the area. Piglet can be found hanging out of Mr. Sanderz tree. Look for Rabbit's sign that reads, "No Bouncing by ORDER of RABBIT (THIS MEANS YOU TIGGER!)" If you feel like getting off of your feet for a while, you can take a break over at Pooh's Thoughtful Spot. If you would rather sulk than rest, then head on over to Eeyore's Gloomy Place. Even though you do not see him, you can also find the entrance to Gopher's house.

7) **Character Meet and Greet Alert!** While still near Pooh's Playful Spot, you can meet some of your favorite friends including Winnie the Pooh, Piglet, Eeyore, and Tigger near the entrance at select times throughout the day.

Fun Fact: Winnie the Pooh may not have made an appearance in Fantasyland until June of 1999, but when he arrived, he replaced two very popular rides. The Many Adventures of Winnie the Pooh is in the same location that Mr. Toad's Wild Ride used to be, while Pooh's Playful Spot is where the popular 20,000 Leagues Under the Sea used to sit.

Epcot

The only reference found in Epcot can be found in **World Showcase**.

8) **Character Meet and Greet Alert!** While at the **United Kingdom** pavilion, you can find that Silly Ol' Bear, Tigger, Piglet, and Eeyore at various times throughout the day doing meet and greets.

Fun Fact: Winnie the Pooh would go on to inspire three more films, The Tigger Movie, Piglet's Big Movie, and Pooh's Heffalump Movie, along with four television shows, Welcome to Pooh Corner, The New Adventures of Winnie the Pooh, The Book of Pooh, and My Friends Tigger and Pooh.

Disney's Hollywood Studios

All of the references in Disney's Hollywood Studios can be found in the **Animation Courtyard**.

9) Super Sleuths Darby, Tigger, and Pooh can be found in action at **Playhouse Disney – Live on Stage!** These characters are based off of the television show "My Friends Tigger and Pooh."

10) There are sketches that demonstrate how to draw Winnie the Pooh on the left hand wall as you exit the **Animation Academy** located inside the **Magic of Disney Animation** building.

Fun Fact: Gopher never appeared in the original Winnie the Pooh stories by A.A. Milne. He even mentions it in the film by stating, "I'm not in the book, you know."

Disney's Animal Kingdom

The sole reference found within Disney's Animal Kingdom is on **Discovery Island** near the entrance to Dinoland, USA.

11) **Character Meet and Greet Alert!** Just before crossing the bridge that leads to Dinoland, USA from **Discovery Island**, you will find a path on your right hand side. Winnie the Pooh, Tigger, Piglet, and Eeyore are at the end of the path doing meet and greets at various times throughout the day.

Fun Fact: Winnie the Pooh and the Blustery Day, the second portion of the film, actually won an Academy Award for Best Animated Short Film in 1968.

Downtown Disney

Winnie the Pooh is the only character on property to have two gift shops inspired by their film. Pooh's Thotful Shop is in Fantasyland and Downtown Disney is the home of **Pooh Corner**, which contains several Winnie the Pooh references.

12) The first references at **Pooh Corner** can be found outside the shop. One is simply Pooh on the sign. The other is statues of Pooh, Piglet, and Tigger found just to the left of the main entrance.

13) After entering **Pooh Corner**, you can find Winnie the Pooh floating with the aid of a balloon above you. You will also notice that Tigger still has not grown fond of trees and is stuck once again. Unfortunately, the narrator is no where to be found to come to his assistance. Also, take a look at the window in the back corner to find a "stuffed animal" Owl on the ledge.

Once Upon a Toy is home to your next reference.

14) While in **Once Upon a Toy**, make your way to the middle room in the store and look at the mural on the wall behind the cash registers. If you look closely, you can find not one, but two stuffed Winnie the Pooh's hidden within the painting.

Your next reference can be found at **Team Mickey**.

15) Tigger and Rabbit are playing basketball near the ceiling on the display in the center of **Team Mickey**.

Make your way to **World of Disney** for a single reference.

16) If you enter **World of Disney** through the entrance below Mickey and Minnie, you will enter a room with several characters hanging from the ceiling. In the back portion of this room, you can find Tigger and Pooh on a flying machine with Piglet hanging on for dear life.

Your final reference at Downtown Disney can be heard while walking through **Downtown Disney's Marketplace**.

17) While walking around **Downtown Disney's Marketplace**, listen for the songs "Rumbly in my Tumbly" and "The Wonderful Thing About Tiggers" from The Many Adventures of Winnie the Pooh. These are two of thirty-two songs that play in the area, so the odds of hearing either of them within the first few songs are pretty slim.

Fun Fact: The Many Adventures of Winnie the Pooh is not the first Disney film to start with the opening of the book. However, it is the first film to have the words of the book present throughout the majority of the film.

Resorts

Your final references to The Many Adventures of Winnie the Pooh can be found at the **Grand Floridian** and **All-Star Movies**.

18) **Character Meet and Greet Alert!** At times, you can find Winnie the Pooh, Tigger, and Piglet at the **1900 Park Fare** character meals at the **Grand Floridian**.

19) While waiting for the buses at **All-Star Movies**, look into the windows of the shop, **Donald's Double Features** to find several Disney characters including Pooh Bear himself!

Fun Fact: Even though Walt Disney passed away eleven years before the film was released, he did get to see Winnie the Pooh before his death in 1966. The first portion of the film, Winnie the Pooh and the Honey Tree, was released February 4, 1966, ten months before Walt's death.

"The Rescuers"

Resorts: June 22, 1977

The Film in Three Paragraphs

The film begins with a little girl dropping a bottle over the side of a boat into the water. We follow the bottle as it travels to New York City and arrives at the Rescue Aid Society, an organization of mice from around the world. When the Society reads the letter, they realize it is from a little girl named Penny who is seeking help. A loving and kind mouse named Miss Bianca and a superstitious mouse named Bernard volunteer to investigate and rescue Penny.

Miss Bianca and Bernard visit Morningside Orphanage, the addressee of the letter, and meet a cat named Rufus who informs them Penny ran away weeks ago. When questioned further, he recalls a woman who owns a pawn shop offering Penny a ride a while back. The two mice go to the pawn shop, find Madame Medusa, and quickly realize she kidnapped Penny. They also learn that Medusa is planning to depart for Devil's Bayou to monitor Penny's Progress in recovering a diamond from a well. The two mice take a flight to Devil's Bayou on an Albatross named Orville.

Upon their arrival, they investigate, locate, and connect with Penny, and quickly form an escape plan with her. Penny is forced down into the well one last time, but this time she returns with the Devil's Eye, the world's largest diamond. As soon as they are back on Medusa's boat, the escape plan goes into effect. Penny takes her teddy bear back from Medusa, which is hiding the Devil's Eye inside. With assistance from the local animals, Bernard, and Bianca, Penny escapes back to her home in New York. Bernard and Bianca are congratulated when they return and become the primary rescuers of the Rescue Aid Society. More importantly, the film concludes with Penny being adopted.

Magic Kingdom

The first reference throughout Walt Disney World can be found on **Main Street, USA**.

1) In the back room of **Exposition Hall**, take a look at the Milestones in Disney Animation on the back wall to find a picture of a very startled looking Bernard.

Fun Fact: This was the first Disney Animated film to have a sequel, 1990's "The Rescuers Down Under."

You can either hop a train or walk to **Mickey's Toontown Fair** for your next reference.

2) **That's Debatable!** Just before entering the kitchen in **Minnie's Country House**, there is a letter from a child named Penny on a corkboard. I believe this is a reference to Penny from "The Rescuers" due to the simple fact that Penny points out in the film that "Mice can talk like anybody." Since the letter is to Minnie, a mouse, and the letter is from a girl named Penny who is talking to a mouse, it leads me to believe that this letter is acknowledging the film. It is your own personal opinion if you think otherwise, but I give this one a huge yes!

The last reference in the Magic Kingdom can be found during the **Celebrate A Dream Come True Parade**.

3) During the **Celebrate A Dream Come True Parade,** you can find Bernard and Bianca on Aladdin's float below Dumbo. They are very difficult to see, but are a great find when you spot them.

Fun Fact: The film was based off a series of books written by Margery Sharp that were part of "The Rescuers" series.

Downtown Disney

The only two references found throughout Downtown Disney are within **World of Disney.**

4) The mural on the ceiling in the "Bird Room" in **World of Disney** contains Orville, Bernard, and Bianca flying overhead. How can you tell it is Orville and not Wilbur from "The Rescuers Down Under?" Even though they both used sardine cans for the passenger seats, Orville wore a purple scarf!

5) While in the same room in **World of Disney,** continue to observe the ceiling. If you look to the lower right hand side of Orville, you can find Evinrude on a branch. This is the only spot throughout all of Walt Disney World where you can find my favorite dragonfly.

Resorts

The final reference to the film is at **All-Star Movies.**

6) While waiting for the buses at **All-Star Movies,** look into the windows at the shop, **Donald's Double Features,** to find several Disney characters including Bernard and Bianca!

Fun Fact: This film was the highest grossing animated film of all time during its initial release.

"The Fox and the Hound"

Released: July 10, 1981

The Film in Three Paragraphs

The film begins with Big Mama, an owl, finding a toddler fox whose mother had just been shot. Big Mama and her two friends Dinky and Boomer, bring the fox to the attention of an old woman named Widow Tweed. She takes the fox in and names him Tod. Meanwhile, Amos Slade, Widow Tweed's next door neighbor, picks up a new hunting dog which he names Copper.

Soon Tod the fox and Copper the hound dog meet and instantly become the best of friends. Unfortunately, Amos' other dog, Chief, finds Tod and creates a ruckus chasing Tod all around the yard and into the chicken coop. Amos promises Widow Tweed that the next time Tod enters his yard, he will be a dead fox. The following day, Amos leaves on a hunting trip with Copper and Chief for several months. When they return, Copper understands that he and Tod are suppose to be enemies. While the two are talking, Chief finds Tod once again, chases him, and in the process falls from a cliff and breaks his leg. Copper, upset by the events, declares he will get his revenge against Tod.

To avoid any future problems, Widow Tweed returns Tod to the forest where he falls in love with a female fox named Vixey. However, Amos develops a plan to finally kill Tod. Amos takes Copper into the forest. After finding and chasing Tod to the top of a cliff, a bear attacks all three of them. Just before the bear kills Copper, Tod comes to the rescue. To return the favor, Copper stands in the line of fire as Amos attempts to shoot Tod. In the end, the two best friends remain separated with only their child memories of the good times they had uniting them in spirit.

Magic Kingdom

The first of only three references found throughout all of Walt Disney World can be found on **Main Street, USA.**

1) The Milestones in Disney Animation in the backroom of **Exposition Hall** contains a picture of Tod and Copper when they are still the best of friends.

Fun Fact: The film was based off a book written by Daniel P. Mannix, which was also entitled, "The Fox and the Hound."

Disney's Hollywood Studios

The next reference to The Fox and the Hound can be found at the **Magic of Disney Animation** in Disney's Hollywood Studios.

2) While waiting in line for the **Magic of Disney Animation,** you can find concept sketches on the walls for several Disney films including one of a young Tod and Copper. If you visit on a day when this area is roped off, ask a cast member if you can take a look around. The majority of the time they are more than happy to help out.

Resorts

The final reference to the film can be found at **All-Star Movies.**

3) While waiting for the buses at **All-Star Movies,** turn around and look at the pictures inside the windows. If you look closely, you can find a film canister which is labeled, "Fox and the Hound."

Fun Fact: The Fox and the Hound was the final Disney animated film to have all of its titles in the opening credits.

"Oliver and Company"

Released: November 18, 1988

The Film in Three Paragraphs

The film begins in New York City with a box full of kittens for sale and eventually each kitten is sold except one. This cat escapes the box, wanders the streets, and helps a dog named Dodger get some hot dogs. Dodger leaves the cat and goes to his hideout where his gang of dogs resides. Unknowingly, the cat follows Dodger and is soon inducted into the gang of dogs.

The leader of the dogs, a man named Fagin, is in debt and trying to earn cash to pay back a man named Sykes. The following day, the gang comes across a limousine as they search for goods to steal in order for Fagin to attain the money to repay his debt. Tito, a Chihuahua, and the cat enter the limo where the cat is discovered by a little girl named Jenny. Jenny adopts the cat and names him Oliver. The gang, fearful Oliver is in pain in his new home, go and "rescue him." Once they return to the hideout, Oliver informs them that he loves Jenny and just wants to go back. When Fagin sees Oliver, however, he forms a plan to hold Oliver for ransom thinking an extremely rich man will pay good money to get his cat back.

After explaining the plan to Sykes, Fagin waits for the rich man, but is stunned to find Jenny in his place. He gives Oliver to her which causes Sykes to kidnap Jenny. The dogs head to Sykes' factory, break in, and escape with Jenny. This results in a high speed car chase through New York City and the death of Sykes. In the end, Oliver remains with Jenny, but still holds his membership as part of Dodger's gang.

Magic Kingdom

The first of only two references in Walt Disney World can be found on **Main Street, USA.**

1) A picture of the original theatrical poster for Oliver and Company can be found in the Milestones of Disney Animation on the back wall in the back room of **Exposition Hall**.

Resorts

The only other reference is at **All-Star Movies**.

2) While waiting for the buses at **All-Star Movies**, take a look at the windows near the entrance to **Donald's Double Features**. Locate Chip and Dale in the right window and take a look at the piece of paper behind them to see the words "Oliver and Company" written out.

Fun Fact: While watching the film, pay attention to the details (much like you would throughout Walt Disney World). Sykes' license plate is "DOBRMAN," and a window in New York City reads "CREDIT DENTIST: O. PAYNE."

"The Little Mermaid"

Released: November 17, 1989

The Film in Three Paragraphs

The film focuses around a little mermaid named Ariel who is fascinated with the human world. Her fish friend, Flounder, and she have a habit of exploring shipwrecks in search for treasures from the human world. Her father, however, is not amused with those "barbarians" and forbids her to go to the surface. While in her treasure trove, some lights from the surface catch Ariel's attention, so she swims to the surface to find a sailing ship that carries a handsome prince named Eric.

The ship gets caught in a storm and Eric is thrown from the boat. Ariel saves him and, like a GPS system, brings him to the beach in his kingdom. The two fall in love instantly, but Ariel swims away before Eric realizes she is a mermaid. Ariel is then approached by Ursula, the evil Sea Witch, about making a bargain. She will make Ariel human in exchange for Ariel's voice. In addition, Ariel must have Eric kiss her within three days or she will become the property of Ursula. Ariel agrees, becomes human, returns to the surface, and meets Eric again. However, since Eric only knew his rescuer by her voice, he does not believe she is the one he is seeking since she can not talk. Ariel and her friends, a crab named Sebastian, Flounder, and a seagull named Scuttle, try to help set the mood so Eric will kiss her and break the spell. Unfortunately, the mood is broken before the kiss.

On the night before Ariel must kiss Eric, Ursula, disguised as a human and using Ariel's voice, approaches Eric. He believes she is the woman he loves since she has Ariel's voice. The two are scheduled to be married the following day. When Scuttle learns the bride to be is the Sea Witch in disguise, Ariel and her friends set out to stop the wedding. Ariel gets her voice back just as the sun sets and Eric realizes it is Ariel he loves. Unfortunately, the three days had passed and Ursula now owns Ariel. Ursula makes a bargain with Ariel's father, King Triton, to give her his kingdom in exchange for Ariel's freedom. King Triton agrees and becomes her prisoner. Luckily, Eric then kills Ursula, which in turn frees all of her prisoners including King Triton. In the end, Eric and Ariel are married and live happily ever after on land.

Magic Kingdom

Your first two references can be found on **Main Street, USA**.

1) As usual, your first reference can be found in the Milestones in Disney Animation display in the backroom of **Exposition Hall**. One picture shows Ariel with several seahorses from the "Under the Sea" segment of the film.

Underneath is a description explaining why The Little Mermaid is considered to be a milestone in Disney Animation.

2) One of the outside windows of the **Emporium** includes a scene from The Little Mermaid featuring Flounder, Sebastian, and, of course, Ariel!

Swim over to **Fantasyland** for your next references.

3) While standing in line for **Mickey's Philharmagic**, take a look at the coming attractions to the theatre. One of the posters includes a picture of Ariel and her sisters and reads, "Ariel's Coral Group: A Must Sea!"

4) During **Mickey's Philharmagic**, you can find Ariel and Flounder in a new version of "Part of Your World" featuring Donald Duck!

Fun Fact: The original animator of Ariel, Glen Keane, animated Ariel in Mickey's Philharmagic, which was the first time the character could be seen in computer animated form.

5) **Character Meet and Greet Alert!** You can meet Ariel herself near the back of Fantasyland at **Ariel's Grotto!** There is also a statue of Ariel in the play area.

6) Adjacent to Ariel's Grotto is **Scuttle's Landing**, which serves frozen drinks. At the top of the tent that houses this stand is Scuttle himself.

Your next reference can be found in **Mickey's Toontown Fair**.

7) There are a few letters on the front table in **Mickey's Country House** including one from Ariel with a return address of "Under the Sea."

The remaining references found within the Magic Kingdom are during the **Fireworks and Parades**.

8) Ariel and Eric are waving to the crowd from the Princess float at the end of the **Celebrate A Dream Come True Parade**.

9) **SpectroMagic** has several references to The Little Mermaid making the parade a must "sea!" You can find Ursula ahead of a float carrying Sebastian, Ariel, Flounder, and King Triton about halfway through the parade.

10) During **Wishes**, several Disney characters make wishes including Ariel.

Fun Fact: In Hans Christian Andersen's original story of The Little Mermaid, Ariel actually had her tongue cut out so she could not speak once on land. Disney decided to take a more magical and less painful approach.

Epcot

The only reference found throughout Epcot can be found in **World Showcase**.

11) **Character Meet and Greet Alert!** If you attend the Princess Storybook Breakfast at **Norway**'s restaurant **Akershus**, you can see that Ariel's wish of being where the humans are has finally come true.

Fun Fact: The film won an Academy Award for Best Original Score, and "Under the Sea" won an Academy Award for Best Original Song.

Disney's Hollywood Studios

Your first group of references at Disney's Hollywood Studios can be found in the **Animation Courtyard**.

12) While waiting in line for the **Magic of Disney Animation**, you can find concept art on the walls for various Disney films. Here you will see how far Ursula, Flotsam, and Jetsam came from the early stages of development to the final product of the film. If the area is roped off, ask a cast member if you can a look around. They are usually more than willing to help you out!

13) While your host talks at the beginning of the **Magic of Disney Animation** show, the screen shows several Disney animated characters from different films. Watch closely to see Ursula in one scene and Ariel with Flounder in another.

14) Also during the **Magic of Disney Animation** show, the host will discuss how they bring a character's movements to life. During this part of the film, a clip of Ursula and her pet eels, Flotsam and Jetsam, are shown on the screen.

15) After exiting the **Magic of Disney Animation** show, you can find two desk areas on your left hand side. The first one has a bulletin board full of pictures from The Little Mermaid including pictures of Ariel, Flounder, and Sebastian.

16) You can paint Flounder in the **Digital Ink and Paint** game located in the **Magic of Disney Animation** building.

17) **The Sound Stage**, an interactive game in the **Magic of Disney Animation**, is hosted by Ursula. The point? To take your voice of course! During her introduction, scenes from the film are shown including one where Ursula takes Ariel's voice.

18) Is your personality similar to Ariel or Ursula? These are two of the possible results for the **You're a Character** game in the **Magic of Disney Animation** building. Please note that you may not get Ariel or Ursula, but if your goal is to have either character in the end, try to answer the questions as they would.

Fun Fact: With the Disney animated films not being as successful as they used to, Disney moved their animation department to trailers off Studio property. This motivated the animators to come back in full force and develop a remarkable film in The Little Mermaid.

19) Before entering the **Voyage of the Little Mermaid** building, check out the billboard outside which shows Ariel, Flounder, Sebastian, Ursula, and King Triton. There is also a three dimensional version above the Fastpass distribution machines.

20) During the **Voyage of the Little Mermaid**, actual scenes from the film are shown along with several characters in puppet and human form. Some of the characters included are Ariel, Prince Eric, Ursula, Flotsam, Jetsam, Sebastian, Flounder, King Triton, and Max. This is one of the few times you can see Eric's dog in real life! You can also hear famous songs from the film including "Poor Unfortunate Souls," "Part of Your World," and, of course, "Under the Sea."

21) The pictures above some of the displays at the shop **In Character** are "pencil" sketchings of Ariel which show the correct way to draw her!

22) On the back wall in the last room in **Walt Disney: One Man's Dream** is an ensemble of pictures from Disney films. One of the films displayed is The Little Mermaid, which is represented by Ariel and a number of seahorses from the "Under the Sea" scene.

After leaving the Animation Courtyard area, head over to **Sunset Boulevard** for your next references.

23) There is a wonderful carving of Ursula on one of the walls in the store **Sweet Spells**.

24) The outside windows of **Sweet Spells** contains an advertisement for Fantasmic! which shows Ursula with her villain friends.

Fun Fact: One of the film's animators estimated drawing approximately eight billion bubbles for the film.

The final group of references in Disney's Hollywood Studios can be found during the nighttime show, **Fantasmic!**

25) Before **Fantasmic!** even begins, you can find two references to the film in the Hollywood Hills Amphitheatre. Both references are found in the seating arrangements. You have the opportunity to sit in Sebastian or Ursula's section. Neither of these seating sections provides the best seating in the theatre, but it may be worth having your picture taken with the signs featuring the two.

26) During the "Dancing Bubbles" sequence of **Fantasmic!** you can find Sebastian, Flounder, and other characters from the "Under the Sea" portion of the film dancing to an instrumental version of the same song.

27) After the "Dancing Bubbles" scene in **Fantasmic!** you will see a ship stuck in a storm on the water screen. Does the ship look familiar to you? It should! It is Prince Eric's ship caught up in a storm.

28) During the "Princess Medley" sequence of **Fantasmic!** you can find Ariel and Prince Eric on their own water float while the song "Part of Your World" plays overhead.

29) Just after the Queen from Snow White and the Seven Dwarfs transforms into the Hag in **Fantasmic!** she calls upon all the forces of evil. In response to her call, Ursula appears on the water screen and can then be found throughout the rest of the sequence with the villains.

30) The final reference to The Little Mermaid during **Fantasmic!** occurs at the very end of the show. You can find both Eric and Ariel on board Steamboat Willie's ship as it sails by.

Fun Fact: Ariel, Sebastian, and Flounder were also present during the Disney Stars and Motor Cars Parade, which ran for almost seven years from 2001 through 2008 in Disney's Hollywood Studios.

Downtown Disney

31) If you head towards the back entrance of **Once Upon a Toy**, take a look at the window on the right hand side to find six of the Disney princesses including everyone's favorite mermaid, Ariel.

32) While at **Downtown Disney Marketplace's Guest Relations** you can find a framed picture of Ariel hanging on the wall.

Fun Fact: The names of Ariel's sisters are Aquata, Alana, Andrina, Adella, Arista, and Attina. In the mermaid world these are practically equivalent to Jenny and Patrick.

The next group of references can be found at and around **World of Disney** in Downtown Disney.

33) Just prior to entering **World of Disney** through the entrance that faces the parking lot, head a few windows to the left of the entrance to find a rather large picture of the ever popular Sea Witch, Ursula.

34) After entering **World of Disney** through the entrance near Ursula, take a look up in the first room to find Ariel and Flounder together high on the ceiling.

35) Pay attention to the detail on the walls in the "Villains Room" in **World of Disney**. Each wall has portraits of different villains, which only appear from a particular angle. One of these portraits changes between Ursula and Jafar. In front of this portrait is the statue of the extremely beautiful Ursula. Below the statue, in the watch display case, are some of Ursula's negotiators that could not fulfill their end of the bargain.

36) While in "Princess Hall" in **World of Disney**, look at the back wall to find some stained glass windows of castles. The third castle over is King Triton's.

37) On the opposite end of the room from the stained glass windows in **World of Disney** is a huge banner above the exit which reads, "Happily Ever After," and features a picture of Ariel.

38) While walking around **Downtown Disney's Marketplace**, listen for the song "Under the Sea" playing overhead. Note that this is not the film version from the song, but is actually sung by a different artist.

39) Ariel and Flounder can be found near one of the big screen televisions in the main dining area of **Planet Hollywood** in **Downtown Disney's West Side**.

Fun Fact: While the studio was working on a script for the film in the 1980's, they came across a basic storyline for The Little Mermaid that Walt Disney himself was working on in 1941. Unfortunately, World War II occurred and seized all hope of the film coming out during his life time.

Resorts

The Little Mermaid has made an appearance in more resorts than most of the Disney animated films. The first resorts you can find a reference at are **Fort Wilderness, Contemporary, Polynesian,** and the **Grand Floridian.**

40) One of the most overlooked experiences throughout Walt Disney World is the **Electric Water Pageant** performed on the Seven Seas Lagoon and can be seen from **Fort Wilderness, Contemporary, Polynesian,** and the **Grand Floridian.** During the pageant, you can hear an instrumental version of "Poor Unfortunate Souls" while an octopus appears on the water. You can also hear the song, "Fathoms Below" playing as the last float passes by. The King that is aboard the last float is not King Triton, Ariel's father, but King Neptune.

The next resort to have a reference is the **Beach Club.**

41) While at the **Beach Club,** look around for a bronzed Ariel on a rock found next to a Disney Vacations Club sign outside of the lobby.

The final references to The Little Mermaid found in Walt Disney World are at **All-Star Music** and **All-Star Movies.**

42) Ariel is playing a guitar with Sebastian and Flounder beside her at the Piano Pool at **All-Star Music.** These three are not within the pool so you do not need to get wet if you want a picture with the three of them.

43) While waiting for the buses at **All-Star Movies,** look into the windows at **Donald's Double Features** to find several Disney characters in a mural including Ariel!

Fun Fact: The song "Part of Your World" was almost never part of the movie.

"DuckTales: The Movie: Treasure of the Lost Lamp"

Released: August 3, 1990

The Film in Three Paragraphs

After Scrooge McDuck finds a map leading to the treasure of Collie Baba, he hires a guide, Dijon, to lead him across the desert. Dijon, however, is working for a great magician named Merlock who wants a magic lamp that is part of the treasure. When Scrooge finds the lamp, he thinks it is a piece of junk and gives it to his nanny's granddaughter, Webby. Dijon turns on Scrooge, and he and Merlock escape with the treasure.

When Scrooge arrives back in Duckburg, Webby realizes the lamp is in fact magical and she and Scrooge's nephews begin to use all of their wishes. Meanwhile, Merlock realizes the lamp is not with the treasure, so he transforms himself into a bird and flies him and Dijon to Duckburg. The children finally come clean about the magic lamp to their Uncle who instantly makes a wish of recovering the treasure of Collie Baba. To celebrate, Scrooge attends a party with the lamp in hand to brag about his newest find.

Unfortunately for Scrooge, Merlock tracks him to the party. Scrooge runs out of the party, but crashes into a cart with another lamp and mistakenly takes that lamp instead. Dijon, realizing the mistake, grabs the actual lamp and wishes for Scrooge's fortune. Scrooge eventually breaks into his money bin to reclaim the lamp, but Merlock gets his hands on the lamp instead and transforms Scrooge's money bin into a flying fortress. After a battle in the sky, Scrooge finally gets everything back to normal. In the end, Scrooge wishes that the Genie will turn into a real boy, and the misadventures finally come to a halt.

Magic Kingdom

The first reference to the film and the DuckTales stories can be found in **Mickey's Toontown Fair**.

1) Besides being home to the world's richest duck, Duckburg holds fame as being the home of Duckburg University, the college Mickey Mouse roots for. Head over to **Mickey's Country House** to see pennants, a football helmet, and a foam finger sporting the Duckburg U. logo in Mickey's living room.

Fun Fact: Prior to the film, 100 episodes of DuckTales had aired making the film the official end of the series.

Disney's Animal Kingdom

The only reference to the film at Disney's Animal Kingdom actually occurs before entering the **park entrance**.

2) **Character Meet and Greet Alert!** At times you can meet Launchpad McQuack at the **park entrance**. Please take note that it is a very rare occurrence to find Launchpad. If he is there, he is typically behind the planters on the right hand side while walking towards the entrance.

Fun Fact: The film introduced a new film label, Disney MovieToons. There was only one other Disney film to use this label: 1995's "A Goofy Movie."

Resorts

The final reference to the film can be found in **All-Star Movies**.

3) If you stop by **Donald's Double Features,** the shop inside **All-Star Movies,** you can find two film canisters at the entrance. The one on the bottom reads, "DuckTales: The Movie" and has the date 1990 just below the title.

Fun Fact: Disney originally planned on having a series of Duck-Tales movies. Due to a low box office turn out, however, the idea was dropped.

"The Rescuers Down Under"

Released: November 16, 1990

The Film in Three Paragraphs

When Marahute, a giant golden eagle, is caught in a poacher trap, a young boy named Cody helps free her. Marahute gives Cody a golden feather to thank him. After Cody leaves her he comes across a mouse in a trap. As he releases the mouse, Cody becomes caught in a trap set by a poacher named Percival C. McLeach. McLeach arrives to learn that he has captured Cody instead of an animal. He is about to release the boy when he notices Marahute's golden feather. He questions Cody on where he found it. When Cody refuses to talk, McLeach kidnaps Cody and takes him back to his hideout.

The mouse who Cody rescued witnesses the entire inci-dent and sends a message to the Rescue Aid Society in New York City. Bernard and Bianca set off to Australia to rescue Cody via Wilbur, Orville's brother from "The Rescuers." Once they arrive, a kangaroo rat named Jake assumes the role of tour guide. Back at McLeach's hideout, McLeach decides the best way to locate Marahute is by releasing Cody and claiming that the bird is dead. McLeach points out to Cody that Marahute's eggs will not survive without their mother with the intent that Cody will go to rescue them and in turn, reveal Marahute's nest to him. Just as he releases Cody, Bernard, Bianca, and Jake see the boy leave, and they hop on board McLeach's truck as it follows Cody.

Once Cody reaches Marahute's nest, the three heroes warn him of the trap, but it is too late. Marahute, along with Cody, Bianca, and Jake, are trapped. The only hope they have is Bernard coming to the rescue. Bernard makes the long trek after McLeach's truck and finally reaches it at the edge of a cliff where McLeach is planning to feed Cody to the crocodiles. Bernard uses his brains to knock McLeach off the cliff and rescue Cody. In the end, Bernard proposes to Bianca, and they soar off into the moonlight on Marahute.

Magic Kingdom

The only reference in the Magic Kingdom can be found during the **Celebrate A Dream Come True Parade**.

1) During the **Celebrate A Dream Come True Parade**, you can find Bernard and Bianca on the float with Aladdin. They are directly below Dumbo and are best seen on the right hand side of the float. This is the same reference as reference number three in 1977's The Rescuers.

Fun Fact: Even though the film was successful, it grossed the least amount of money of any of the Disney animated films that were released between 1989 and 1999.

Epcot

The next reference can be found at **Soarin'** which is located in **The Land** pavilion.

2) While waiting in line for **Soarin'** pay attention to the music that is played. At various times you can hear the theme song for The Rescuers Down Under.

Disney's Hollywood Studios

The two remaining references for The Rescuers Down Under can be found in the **Animation Courtyard** area of Disney's Hollywood Studios.

3) While waiting in line for the **Magic of Disney Animation**, you can find a piece of concept art featuring Cody hugging Marahute on a wall. If you visit on a day when this area is roped off, ask a cast member if you can take a look around. They are often more than willing to assist.

4) The final reference to The Rescuers Down Under can be found in the far back room of **Walt Disney: One Man's Dream**. Just before entering the film, head towards the back wall of the back room to find a picture from the film.

Fun Fact: Orville, voiced by Jim Jordan in "The Rescuers," would have returned in "The Rescuers Down Under," but he passed away a few years earlier. Due to this, Orville was given a brother, Wilbur (just like the Wright Brothers), who was voiced by John Candy.

"Beauty and the Beast"

Released: November 22, 1991

The Film in Three Paragraphs

After a prince turns away a gift of a beautiful rose because the person giving it to him is a hag, she points out that appearances can be deceiving and reveals herself as a beautiful woman. She turns the prince into a beast and casts a spell on his castle where he must find love and have the love returned before his twenty-first year or he shall be a beast forever. Years pass and the audience is introduced to Belle, a beautiful girl in a little town who does not quite fit in. Local pretty boy, Gaston, wants to marry her for her beauty, but she does not return the feelings.

Maurice, Belle's father, gets lost in the woods and comes across a castle, home of the Beast. The Beast is upset with the intruder and locks him away. Belle eventually finds her father and trades places with him in the castle. At first, the Beast repulses her. However, after she escapes and he saves her life, the two begin looking at one another differently. When Belle learns her father is lost in the woods and sick, the Beast releases her so she can save her father. Before she leaves, he gives her a magical mirror so she will always remember him.

Once back at home with her father, Gaston creates an evil plan to wed Belle. He convinces the curator for the Asylum for Loons to commit Maurice unless Belle agrees to marry him. When Gaston explains that Maurice was raving about a Beast to prove he is crazy, Belle counters by showing the villagers the magic mirror and revealing the Beast. Gaston realizes Belle has feelings for the Beast and sets off to kill him. The Beast and Gaston have a battle at the castle. Gaston falls to his death and the Beast is severely wounded. As the Beast is dying, Belle professes her love, which breaks the spell. In the end, the two, according to housekeeper Mrs. Potts, live happily ever after.

Magic Kingdom

Your first reference can be found right away on **Main Street, USA**.

1) There is a picture of Belle looking off dreamily in the back room of **Exposition Hall** in the Milestones in Disney Animation mural. Another picture present is a rough sketch of the Beast at what appears to be the earlier stages of production. Below these pictures is a description explaining why Beauty and the Beast is considered to be a milestone in Disney animation.

Go over to **Fantasyland** for your next four references.

2) **Character Meet and Greet Alert!** Belle is one of the characters that is available to meet during the **Once Upon a Time Character Breakfast** at **Cinderella's Royal Table**.

3) While watching **Mickey's Philharmagic**, you can actually find a 3-D Lumiere performing the ever popular song, "Be Our Guest."

4) From Mickey's Philharmagic, head to the other side of the carousel and stop by **Mrs. Potts' Cupboard** for a wonderful hot fudge sundae. You can find a picture of both Mrs. Potts and Chip on the sign above the entrance to this location.

5) **Character Meet and Greet Alert!** The final reference in Fantasyland is around the corner from Winnie the Pooh and past the Enchanted Grove. Here you will find the **Fairy Tale Garden**. At various times throughout the day, Belle reads a story to the audience and even invites guests to come up and play the parts of her enchanted friends including the Beast!

Fun Fact: The Village Fry Shoppe found in Fantasyland used to be known as Lumiere's Kitchen.

The remaining references in the Magic Kingdom can be found during the **Celebrate A Dream Come True Parade** and the **Fireworks**.

6) Belle and the Beast can be found on the Princess float near the end of the **Celebrate A Dream Come True Parade**.

7) During the Magic Kingdom's nighttime fireworks show, **Wishes**, you can hear Beauty and the Beast music playing during a portion of the show.

Fun Fact: The film inspired two sequels, with both taking place in the middle of the original film.

Epcot

The three references found in Epcot are all located in **World Showcase**.

8) **Character Meet and Greet Alert!** Every morning you can meet Belle during the **Princess Storybook Breakfast** at the restaurant **Akershus** in **Norway**. Note that this is a popular breakfast so make sure you book early in order to attend.

9) **Character Meet and Greet Alert!** You can meet Belle, Beast, and occasionally Gaston from time to time around the **France** pavilion. They are not available the entire day so check with a cast member on when would be a good time to meet them.

10) While still in **France**, stop by the back room of the shop **Plume et Palette** to find the stained glass window that features the same pictures as the one from the beginning of the film. While in the shop, you can also find the Beast's rose in a glass case and a Beauty and the Beast story book entitled, "La Belle et La Bete."

Fun Fact: One of the biggest worries for people working on the film was that Walt Disney himself had attempted the story twice before, but could never get the components right. Everyone had to remind themselves that they were not Walt and in the end, they ended up with a masterpiece.

Disney's Hollywood Studios

Your first reference can be found at the end of **Hollywood Boulevard**.

11) In front of the **Great Movie Ride** are the handprints of Angela Lansbury, the voice of Mrs. Potts. She even included the name of the film and her character's name in the engraving.

The next group of references can be found in the **Animation Courtyard**.

12) While waiting in line for the **Magic of Disney Animation**, you can find a piece of concept art for the film which shows Belle with a werewolf looking Beast. If this part of the line is roped off, ask a cast member if you take a look around. They are typically more than willing to let you.

13) You can find a small figurine of Belle located on the left hand side of the room that the **Magic of Disney Animation** show is shown in.

14) While your host talks about everyone having their own favorite Disney character at the beginning of the **Magic of Disney Animation** show, pay close attention to the screen to find Belle and the Beast pictured together and Cogsworth and Lumiere shown together.

15) Also during the **Magic of Disney Animation** show, your host will discuss how animators bring characters movements to life. During this portion of the show, you can find a very angry looking Beast on the screen behind your host.

16) Have you ever wanted to be a voice of Belle and the Beast? If so, stop by the interactive game **The Sound Stage** in the **Magic of Disney Animation** building. Choose the Act option and then select the scene where everyone's favorite beauty tries to help the Beast after he was attacked by wolves.

17) The **You're a Character** game in the **Magic of Disney Animation** building is hosted by Lumiere and Cogsworth.

In addition, two of the possible outcomes for the game are Cogsworth and Belle. Please note that you may not always get one of these characters, or ever get them, but if your goal is to have either character as the result in the end, try to answer the questions as you believe they would.

18) There are "pencil" sketchings of Belle demonstrating the correct way to draw her above one of the displays in the shop **In Character**.

19) While inside **Walt Disney: One Man's Dream**, head to the far back room and take a look at the back wall, which has an ensemble of pictures from Disney films clumped together. One of the films displayed is Beauty and the Beast and shows the title characters in the famous ballroom scene.

20) There are songs playing throughout all of Walt Disney World. The song "Beauty and the Beast" plays from time to time in the **Animation Courtyard**.

Fun Fact: The Academy Award winning song, "Beauty and the Beast," was sung by a very hesitant Angela Lansbury. She usually sang upbeat songs, while this was slower moving. However, the song we know and love today in the film was actually recorded in the first take.

After leaving the Animation Courtyard, make your way to **Sunset Boulevard** for your next reference.

21) About half way down Sunset Boulevard on your right hand side is the **Beauty and the Beast – Live on Stage** show. All of your favorite characters from the film appear in the show including Belle, Beast, Gaston, Lumiere, and many more. The show has songs from the film including "Belle," "Be Our Guest," "Gaston," "Something There," "The Mob Song," and of course the ever popular, "Beauty and the

Beast." In front of the Theater of the Stars (the theatre where the show takes place), there are banners and signs that feature some of the characters from the film.

At the end of the day at Disney's Hollywood Studios, make sure to check out **Fantasmic!** for several references to Beauty and the Beast.

22) Your first reference at **Fantasmic!** can be found on the pathway leading up to the show. On the left and right hand side of the path are banners of different Disney characters including the Beast.

23) Before getting seated for **Fantasmic!** look at the different seating sections. One of the banners features the Beast.

24) During the Dancing Bubbles sequence of **Fantasmic!** you can find the dancing plates and cups on the water screen followed by Lumiere, Chip, Mrs. Potts, and Cogsworth. An instrumental version of "Be Our Guest" plays overhead to complement the video.

25) You can find Beast and Belle on their own water float while "Beauty and the Beast" plays overhead during the Princess Medley sequence of **Fantasmic!**

26) At the very end of **Fantasmic!** you can find Belle and the Beast on the steamboat with Mickey.

Fun Fact: Howard Ashman, who worked on the songs for the film and The Little Mermaid with Alan Menken, died during production of the film. At the end of the credits is a wonderful tribute to him that reads, "To our friend Howard, who gave a mermaid her voice, and a beast his soul, we will be forever grateful."

Disney's Animal Kingdom

The only Beauty and the Beast reference throughout Disney's Animal Kingdom can be found at **Discovery Island**.

27) While waiting for the doors to open for **it's tough to be a bug**, take a look around at the posters of musicals that have been performed by the bugs. One is titled "Beauty and the Bees." If you are lucky, you may hear the Beauty and the Beast song playing overhead with a slightly buggy twist.

Fun Fact: While watching the film, pay close attention to what the enchanted characters call Belle and you will discover that Chip is the only one who actually calls her by name.

Downtown Disney

28) Your first reference in Downtown Disney can be found near the back entrance to **Once Upon a Toy**. Take a look in the window to the right of the entrance to find a picture of Belle with five of her Disney princess friends.

29) While in **Downtown Disney's Marketplace's Guest Relations**, you can find pictures of several Disney princesses including Belle.

30) If you enter **World of Disney** through the doors below Huey, Dewey, and Louie, you will enter the "Enchanted Dining Room." In the middle of the room are giant statues of Lumiere and Belle greeting you. If you look around the room, you can find several other characters from the film. Please note that the dishes in this room can not tell you if the food is delicious.

31) Make your way to the backroom on the opposite side of **World of Disney** for your next reference. The stained glass windows in the back of the room contain pictures of

several castles within the glass. The second castle from the left belongs to the Beast.

32) Look up and to the right about halfway towards the entrance in the same room of **World of Disney** to find a banner of Belle and the Beast.

33) The final reference in **World of Disney** can be found just above the exit in the same room as the past two clues. Here you can find a banner which reads, "Happily Ever After" and features Belle and seven other Disney princesses.

34) While walking around **Downtown Disney's Marketplace**, listen for the song "Be Our Guest." It is actually sung in French and is one of thirty-two songs played in the area.

Fun Fact: Before the film was released, it was entered into the New York Film Festival. Since the film was not yet completed, parts of the film were only shown with pencil tests!

Resorts

The first resort to feature a Beauty and the Beast references is the **Grand Floridian**.

35) **Character Meet and Greet Alert!** At times you can find Belle at the **1900 Park Fare Character Breakfast** at the **Grand Floridian**. Please note that she is not present all of the time.

36) While in the main lobby of **The Grand Floridian,** you can find a picture of Chip and a picture of Mrs. Potts made out of marble near the entrance to **The Garden View Lounge**.

Your next stop is the **All-Star Resorts**.

37) Not only was Beauty and the Beast the only animated film to be nominated for best picture at the Academy Awards, it also had a Broadway musical based off of it. While at **All-Star Music**, head over to the Broadway section of the resort to see they are currently "showing" none other than Beauty and the Beast!

38) While in the **Intermission** food court at **All-Star Music**, check out the notes in the food court area. If you were to play these musical notes, you would be playing the song "Be Our Guest."

39) When entering the **World Premiere** food court at **All-Star Movies**, take a look at the wall on your left to find an original poster for Beauty and the Beast.

40) While waiting for the buses at **All-Star Movies**, look into the windows of the shop **Donald's Double Features** to find several Disney characters including Belle!

The final reference to Beauty and the Beast can be found at **Pop Century**.

41) There are several shadow boxes in the lobby of **Pop Century**. One of these includes a cell image from Beauty and the Beast as the center piece for the animation and the company in the 1990's. Also in this box is a sketch of Belle and the Beast in the lower left hand corner and a magnet featuring Lumiere!

Fun Fact: After seeing the success of the Star Wars special editions being re-released in theatres in the late 1990's, the Company decided to re-release Beauty and the Beast with a song originally intended for the film, "Human Again."

"Aladdin"

Released: November 25, 1992

The Film in Three Paragraphs

When Jafar tries to retrieve a magical lamp from the Cave of Wonders, he realizes he must use diamond in the rough Aladdin to get it for him. Meanwhile, Princess Jasmine is tired of palace life and escapes into the streets of Agrabah where she meets Aladdin. The two hit it off right away, but soon Aladdin is captured by the city guards and thrown into jail. While in jail, a disguised Jafar confronts Aladdin about going after a treasure to which Aladdin obliges. Once Aladdin has recovered the lamp, Jafar attempts to take it away. Fortunately, thanks to Aladdin's pet monkey Abu, the lamp stays in Aladdin's possession.

Once Aladdin rubs the lamp, a Genie appears and says he will grant him three wishes. His first wish is to become a prince so he can marry Jasmine. After meeting Jasmine as Prince Ali, she turns him away at once. They then take a magic carpet ride, and she realizes he is the one for her. Jafar, however, is not thrilled about Prince Ali and throws him off a cliff. Luckily for Aladdin, Genie arrives and saves Aladdin's life as his second wish. The following day, the Sultan announces that Jasmine and Prince Ali shall be wed. In the meantime, Jafar's henchman, a parrot named Iago, gets control of the lamp.

Jafar quickly makes a wish to become sultan followed by his second wish to be the world's greatest sorcerer. He sends Aladdin away, but thanks to Aladdin's Magic Carpet, he quickly returns. Just when Jafar is about to take control of everything, Aladdin tricks him into using his third wish to become a powerful Genie. Jafar makes the wish and becomes a prisoner of the lamp. Aladdin then uses his final wish to give Genie his freedom. In the end, the Sultan realizes that Aladdin has proved himself worthy of being with his daughter and changes the law so the two can finally live happily ever after.

Magic Kingdom

Grab your Magic Carpet and head off to **Main Street, USA** for the start of your adventure.

1) The back wall of the rear room in **Exposition Hall** shows the Milestones in Disney Animation. One of the pictures shown here is Aladdin and Jasmine taking their final magic carpet ride at the end of the film.

2) Take a look at the **Emporium** windows that face Town Square to find one that portrays a scene from Aladdin.

Your next group of references can be found in **Adventureland**.

3) In the center of Adventureland is the primary reference to the film in this section of the park, **The Magic Carpets of Aladdin**. While the various carpets you can ride are different colors, they all have the same pattern as the carpet in the film. Aladdin's voice, and a Spanish speaking Genie, can be heard before you take off. Also, pay close attention to the hub of the ride to find multiple pictures of Genie on the bottom layer, Abu on the next layer, and the Scarab jewel, which Jafar used to unlock the Cave of Wonders, on the top layer. At the very top of the attraction is the Genie's lamp.

Fun Fact: The Magic Carpets of Aladdin arrived in Adventureland on May 24, 2001.

4) **Character Meet and Greet Alert!** Just after entering Adventureland from Main Street, you can typically find Aladdin, Jasmine, Genie, and Jafar at select times throughout the day near the **Veranda**. If they are not here, they may be near the **Elephant Tales** gift shop.

5) The final reference in Adventureland can be found at **The Enchanted Tiki Room – Under New Management.**

Before heading inside, you can see Iago on the sign out front. After entering the show, Iago and Zazu, from The Lion King, take over the show. Iago even sings a new version of "Friend Like Me."

Fun Fact: The Enchanted Tiki Room in Disneyland was the first attraction to feature Audio-Animatronics, which are now present in most Disney attractions. Iago and Zazu did not join the show until 1998.

Your next group of references can be found in **Fantasyland**.

6) **Character Meet and Greet Alert!** While at **Cinderella's Royal Table's Once Upon a Time Character Breakfast** located inside Cinderella Castle, you can meet Jasmine the majority of the time. Please make reservations far in advance to be able to experience this amazing character meal.

7) While waiting in line for **Mickey's Philharmagic,** take a look at the posters for upcoming shows. One of these posters shows a picture of Genie and reads, "Genie Sings the Blues."

8) During **Mickey's Philharmagic,** you will experience several classic Disney scenes in 3-D with Donald Duck. In one scene, Aladdin and Jasmine ride their Magic Carpet as Donald (and you) give chase. However, Iago comes along and ruins the fun.

Fun Fact: Aladdin originally had a mother in the film, but she was eventually cut since it did not seem to be working. Unfortunately, the song Aladdin would have sung for his mother, "Proud of Your Boy," had to be cut as well.

The final references in the Magic Kingdom can be found during the **Fireworks and Parades**.

9) The Genie, Abu, and Jafar can be found walking behind

Pinocchio's float in the **Celebrate A Dream Come True Parade**.

10) Aladdin rides Magic Carpet with Genie right behind on a flight-themed float during the **Celebrate A Dream Come True Parade**.

11) The final reference in the **Celebrate A Dream Come True Parade** is found on Peter Pan's float. This is a tricky one to see, but very cool once you spot it. If you take a look at the crystal bubbles behind Peter, you will see that one of these contains a crystal Abu.

12) At night, when **SpectroMagic** takes center stage through the streets of Main Street, Liberty Square, and Frontierland, you can find the Genie keeping Goofy on task as they make some music.

Fun Fact: The Genie actually took the place of Roger Rabbit in SpectroMagic. Since the Roger Rabbit craze of the late 1980's was beginning to wear off by the early 1990's, the Genie replaced him and has remained there to this day.

13) During **Wishes**, Aladdin makes a wish for Genie's freedom and later in the show Genie helps grant some wishes.

Fun Fact: In previous Aladdin stories, the Genie would grant an infinite number of wishes; however, the writers of Disney's Aladdin decided it would be better if only a maximum number of three wishes would be granted in the film.

Epcot

You will be shown the world (and some cool Aladdin references) in **World Showcase**.

14) **Character Meet and Greet Alert!** Your first stop on your whole new world tour is **Norway's Akershus** restaurant which offers the **Princess Storybook Breakfast** on a daily basis. Here you can meet Princess Jasmine for breakfast.

15) **Character Meet and Greet Alert!** Explore the back streets of **Morocco** to possibly meet Aladdin, Jasmine, Genie, Abu, and Jafar at select times throughout the day. At times these characters can be found in front of the pavilion as well.

16) While waiting in line to meet the characters from Aladdin in **Morocco**, look around for additional Aladdin references like the Aladdin storybook that sits on the table.

Fun Fact: The Genie never had a desire to be free in any previous adaptations of the Aladdin stories, but in Disney's Aladdin, Genie has the "American Dream" of freedom.

Disney's Hollywood Studios

Your first reference at Disney's Hollywood Studios can be found at the end of **Hollywood Boulevard**.

17) You can find the hand prints of Robin Williams, who provided the voice of the Genie, in front of the replica of Mann's Chinese Theatre, home to the **Great Movie Ride**.

Fun Fact: A car shaped like the Genie was one of the car floats used in the Disney Stars and Motor Cars parade which ran from October 1, 2001 until March 8, 2008.

After checking out Robin Williams' hand prints, head over to the **Animation Courtyard** for several Aladdin references.

18) While waiting in line for the **Magic of Disney Animation**, take a look at the concept sketches for various films on the

walls, including a scene of Aladdin and Jasmine's magic carpet ride. If you visit on a less crowded day, see if a cast member will let you take a look at the closed off sections of the line. They are typically more than willing to help.

19) The next reference can be found in the room where the **Magic of Disney Animation** show with Mushu takes place. If you take a look behind the drawing of Mushu on the desk, you can find a statue of Aladdin riding Carpet on the third shelf up on the right hand side.

20) While in the same room in the **Magic of Disney Animation,** look at the shelves on the right hand side of the room to find a statue of Jafar in a glass case.

21) While your host talks about everyone having their own favorite character at the beginning of the **Magic of Disney Animation** show, watch the screen to catch a glimpse of Aladdin, the Genie, and Jafar.

22) Just after you exit the **Magic of Disney Animation** show, you will walk past two offices on your left hand side. Just below the bulletin board that is filled with Little Mermaid references in the first room, you will see that this particular artist has visited the **Animation Academy** during an "Iago" session.

23) You can "paint" Iago by playing the **Digital Ink and Paint** game located in the **Magic of Disney Animation.**

24) Have you ever wanted to be the voice of Jafar or Iago? While in the **Magic of Disney Animation** building, play the interactive game **The Sound Stage** and choose the "Act" option. You will then have the opportunity to put your voice into the scene where Jafar and Iago discuss finding the "diamond in the rough."

25) Is your personality similar to Aladdin or Jafar? These two are two of the possible results in the **You're a Character** game in the **Magic of Disney Animation** building. Please note that you may not always get or ever get Aladdin or Jafar, but if your goal is to end up with either of these two, try to answer the questions as you believe they would.

Fun Fact: Originally Aladdin was going to be much younger, but the animators decided that Jasmine would not want to be with a younger guy.

26) Look at the pictures above some of the displays in the shop **In Character** to find "pencil" sketchings of Jasmine that demonstrate the correct way to draw her!

27) On the back wall in the last room in **Walt Disney: One Man's Dream** are a group of overlapping pictures from Disney films. One of the pictures shows Aladdin with Genie, Abu, and the Magic Carpet.

Fun Fact: While the outline of Carpet was drawn, the design on the character was added by a computer so it would remain consistent throughout the entire film. Some of the objects located within his pattern are the lamp, the scarab beetle that led Jafar to the Cave, and the Cave of Wonders itself.

Once you have found all of the references in the **Animation Courtyard**, head on over to **Sunset Boulevard** for your next references.

28) In the connected stores **Sweet Spells** and **Villains In Vogue** is a carving of Jafar high on one of the walls. Also, one of the center displays is Jafar in snake form!

29) After finding the references within **Sweet Spells** and **Villains In Vogue**, go outside and look in one of the windows to find an advertisement for Fantasmic! which features Jafar, once again, as a snake.

Your final group of references within Disney's Hollywood Studios can be found during **Fantasmic!**

30) While walking on the pathway to the Hollywood Hills Amphitheatre, the theatre where **Fantasmic!** takes place, you can find several banners of different Disney characters. One of these banners features Jafar, who also has his own section in the theatre!

31) During the "Dancing Bubbles" segment of **Fantasmic!** you can find the Genie dancing along to an instrumental version of "Never Had a Friend Like Me."

32) The Magic Carpet gives Aladdin and Princess Jasmine a magical ride on the water screen during the "Princess Medley" portion of **Fantasmic!**

33) Just after the Queen from Snow White transforms into the Hag in **Fantasmic!** she calls upon all the forces of evil. In response to her call, Jafar is one of the villains that appear on the water screen. Jafar decides to get rid of Mickey by sending him into the Cave of Wonders, which appears on the water screen. Mickey then rides on the Magic Carpet while desperately trying to escape the Cave of Wonders.

34) After Mickey goes through the Cave of Wonders in **Fantasmic!** Jafar transforms into a gigantic snake and chases Mickey around on stage. Mickey escapes the sticky situation by rubbing a magic lamp, which turns Jafar into a Genie on the water screen.

35) At the very end of **Fantasmic!** you can find Aladdin and Jasmine on the steamboat with Mickey.

Fun Fact: Although the Tiger's head that is the entrance to the Cave of Wonders is not an actual character, it holds the honor of being the first animated head used in a Disney film that was made by computer generation.

Disney's Animal Kingdom

The only reference found throughout Disney's Animal Kingdom can be found during **Mickey's Jammin' Jungle Parade**.

36) It appears that the Genie is still seeing the world after his new found freedom. It looks like he has taken some inspiration from the Goofy hat he wears at the end of the film since his lamp can be found on the hood of Goofy's car during **Mickey's Jammin' Jungle Parade**.

Fun Fact: The voice of Jafar, Jonathon Freeman, actually had a fear of birds. This would not have been a problem, but during some recording sessions they had a parrot (representing Iago) in the room with him so he could react to it.

Downtown Disney

Your first reference in the Marketplace is located at **Disney's Days of Christmas**.

37) You can find Disney's version of the classic "12 Days of Christmas" song on the inside and outside of **Disney's Days of Christmas**. On the ninth day of Christmas, true love has given the gift of Nine Genie's Flying. You can find Genie in several forms on the wall next to the plaque, along with his trusty ol' lamp.

38) Take a look at the windows to the right of the back entrance of **Once Upon a Toy** to find a picture of Jasmine and five of her princess friends.

39) While still outside of **Once Upon a Toy**, take a step back towards the fountain and look above the back section of the store. Coming out of the chimney is none other than the Genie himself!

40) While at **Downtown Disney's Marketplace's Guest Relations,** you can find several princesses in portraits including the always lovely Jasmine.

41) If you enter **World of Disney** through the entrance that is below Mickey and Minnie, you will enter a room with several Disney characters hanging from the ceiling. Here you can find Aladdin, Jasmine, Iago, Abu, and Carpet flying overhead.

42) While in the same room of **World of Disney**, take a look at the murals that are on the walls near the ceiling. In the back part of the room is a scene where Mickey and Minnie are flying on Carpet with Aladdin, Jasmine, and Abu over Agrabah.

43) Take a look at the ceiling of the "Magic Room" in **World of Disney** to find several Disney characters that are associated with magic. The Genie and his lamp can be found in one of the panels.

44) From the "Magic Room" of **World of Disney**, head back across the room in clues 41 and 42 and enter the "Villains Room." While here look at the portraits of villains on the walls to find one that switches between Ursula and Jafar.

45) Make your way to the scrap booking room in **World of Disney** to find Genie, with camera in hand, in the center of the room!

46) Take a look at the ceiling in the "Bird Room" inside **World of Disney** to find several Disney animals including one of my favorite sidekicks, Iago. Notice that Iago is near Zazu in the mural marking the second time these two can be found in the same spot throughout the Walt Disney World Resort.

47) The back wall of "Princess Hall" in **World of Disney** has several castles in a stained glass window. One of these castles belongs to Princess Jasmine's father, the Sultan.

48) While facing the exit of **World of Disney** in "Princess Hall," look to the right hand side near the ceiling to find banners of different Disney couples including one of Jasmine and Aladdin.

49) The final reference in **World of Disney** can be found on the banner above the exit in "Princess Hall" which reads, "Happily Ever After." Jasmine is on the sign with seven of her princess friends.

50) While walking around **Downtown Disney's Marketplace**, listen for the song "Never Had a Friend Like Me." This is one of thirty-two songs that play in the area so the odds of hearing it right away are pretty slim.

Fun Fact: The film contains several references to past Disney films. Examples include the Genie turns his head into Pinocchio's, Genie also pulls Sebastian out of a book, he also uses the word "Dumbo" in Abu's transformation into an elephant, and the Beast is one of the Sultan's toys.

Downtown Disney Westside

All of your Aladdin references on Downtown Disney's Westside can be found in **DisneyQuest**.

51) Just after entering **DisneyQuest**, but before boarding the elevators, take a look at the top of the pillars in the center of the room. One of the characters found here is Jafar.

52) Just after passing the turnstiles in **DisneyQuest**, you will enter an elevator where the Genie welcomes you and goes through a hilarious spiel. As soon as the elevator opens, check out the Genie cut out that is perfect for photo opportunities.

53) Have you ever wanted to control how Magic Carpet flies? Now you can! The interactive game **Aladdin's Magic Carpet Ride** in **DisneyQuest** provides the opportunity to hop aboard Magic Carpet for a high flying mission.

Resorts

The final references to Aladdin can be found at **All-Star Movies** and **Pop Century**.

54) You can find a picture full of Disney characters including Aladdin in the window behind the bus stop at **All-Star Movies**. If you look at the next window over, you can also find the Genie's lamp within the prop box.

55) While at **Pop Century**, take a look at the shadow box in the main lobby that depicts Disney films from the 1990's. Here you will find a magnet of the film's original poster and toys of the Genie, Aladdin with Abu, and Jasmine with Rajah. You can find a picture of Aladdin here as well.

Fun Fact: The story of Aladdin did not end with the movie. The film inspired a television show and two sequels, "The Return of Jafar" and "Aladdin and the King of Thieves."

"The Lion King"

Released: June 24, 1994

The Film in Three Paragraphs

Everyone is excited when the future king of the Pride Lands, Simba, is born. His Uncle Scar is upset, however, since he is no longer heir to the throne. Time passes and Simba's father,

Mufasa, shows Simba his future kingdom and points out a forbidden territory that Simba must never go to. When Simba learns it is an elephant graveyard, his best friend Nala and him decide to explore the area. While at the graveyard, hyenas attack them, but luckily Mufasa comes to the rescue. Mufasa tells Simba that even though he may not always be with him on earth, he will always be watching from the stars where the great kings of the past reside.

Scar conceives a plan to get rid of both Simba and Mufasa by leading Simba into a gorge and telling him to remain there. Scar has the hyenas create a stampede through the gorge and then tells Mufasa that Simba is trapped. Mufasa comes to the rescue, saves Simba, but Scar then flings Mufasa back into the stampede where he falls to his death. Scar convinces Simba that Mufasa's death was Simba's fault and that he should run away. Simba runs into the desert and eventually passes out. He is then rescued by a warthog named Pumba and meerkat named Timon who show Simba a life of forgetting the past and relaxing without a care in the world.

Simba grows up and a desperate Nala comes across him, Timon, and Pumba. When Nala realizes it is Simba, she tries to convince him to return to the Pride Lands. Simba, convinced that his father's death was his fault, refuses to return. A baboon named Rafiki allows Simba to see a vision of his father who tells Simba that he must return home. Simba, convinced that his kingdom needs him, returns home and defeats Scar. In the end, Nala and him have a child of their own, which brings the story to a full circle.

Magic Kingdom

Your Hakuna Matata trip begins on **Main Street, USA**.

1)   The Milestones in Disney Animation, which can be found in the back room of **Exposition Hall**, has a picture of Rafiki holding up baby Simba. Underneath the picture is a description explaining why The Lion King is considered a milestone.

Your next reference is located in **Adventureland**.

2)   Adventureland is the location of Zazu's new home, **The Enchanted Tiki Room – Under New Management**. Before you enter, you can find Zazu on the sign out front. Once inside, you will watch business partners Zazu and Iago (from Aladdin) take over the show.

Fantasyland has had a connection with The Lion King since the film was first released, so stop by to see what the current connection is.

3)   Both Simba and Zazu sing "I Just Can't Wait to be King" during **Mickey's Philharmagic**. The song is shortened, and Donald Duck has been added, but it is a great chance to catch these characters in 3-D.

Fun Fact: Before Mickey's Philharmagic had a place in Fantasyland, a show based off The Lion King named Legend of The Lion King was in the same location.

Fun Fact: Notice that Zazu is an extremely short walk from "it's a small world," home to the song with the same name which he sang in the film to annoy Scar.

The final references in the Magic Kingdom can be found during the **Celebrate A Dream Come True Parade**.

4)   Peter Pan's float in the **Celebrate A Dream Come True Parade** has two Lion King references. If you look behind Peter, you can find a statue of Simba in crystallized form. For the second reference, look at the "merry-go-round" portion of the float to find Timon.

Fun Fact: If you watch the film closely, you will realize that many scenes are paralleled throughout the film including: (1) Nala pins Simba twice, (2) Simba escapes from the Pride Lands through thorns and when he returns to who he truly is, he goes through vines, and (3) Rafiki holds Simba at the start of the film and Simba's daughter at the end of the film.

Epcot

The only two references to the film in Epcot can be found in **Future World**.

5) **The Land** pavilion is home to the **Circle of Life** show. Before entering the show, you can find signs inside the building featuring Timon and Pumba pointing out where to go. The show itself is hosted by Timon, Pumba, and Simba.

6) While still in **The Land** pavilion, stop by the **KidCot** spot. Pumba and Timon are the spokesmen for this specific Kid-Cot station.

Fun Fact: The start of The Lion King was originally planned to have dialogue. After the famous "Circle of Life" sequence was created, the directors of the film realized a musical number was a better introduction to the story.

Disney's Hollywood Studios

The majority of the references to the film in Disney's Hollywood Studios are located in the **Animation Courtyard**.

7) While in line for the **Magic of Disney Animation**, you can find two pieces of concept artwork for The Lion King. One picture features Simba, Timon, and Pumba living their Hakuna Matata lifestyle, and the second picture shows Rafiki holding up Simba. If you arrive on a day when this area is roped off, ask a cast member if you can take a look around.

8) At the beginning of the **Magic of Disney Animation** show, watch the screen behind your host. If you watch closely, you can find Timon and Pumba together, Scar by himself, and Simba by himself.

9) During the **Magic of Disney Animation** show, your host discusses how the animators bring a character's movements to life. During this part of the film, a series of clips from various Disney films appear on the screen including one of Zazu.

10) While waiting in line to meet The Incredibles in the **Magic of Disney Animation** building, you can find a playground styled game with the objective to mix and match body parts of different Disney characters. One of the characters found here is Timon.

11) You can "paint" Timon in the interactive game **Digital Ink and Paint** while you are in the **Magic of Disney Animation** building.

12) Have you ever wanted to provide the voice for Simba and Scar? While in the **Magic of Disney Animation** building you can! Try out the interactive game **The Sound Stage** and choose Act! After you have selected "Act," you can put your voice into the scene where Simba learns about the Elephant Graveyard.

13) While still at **The Sound Stage** game in the **Magic of Disney Animation** building, select "Sing" to provide the voices of Simba, Timon, and Pumba for the song "Hakuna Matata."

14) Is your personality similar to Nala's? You can find out by playing the **You're a Character** game in the **Magic of Disney Animation** building. Please take note that you may not always get Nala, or ever get her, but if your goal is to have her as the result in the end, try to answer the questions as you believe she would.

15) While waiting in line for the **Animation Academy** inside the **Magic of Disney Animation** building, take a look at the character pencil sketches on the wall as one is a young Simba.

Fun Fact: While The Lion King was in production, many thought it would be outperformed by Pocahontas. Therefore, many of the more talented artists were assigned to Pocahontas due to the expectation that it would bring in a larger audience and more money. Instead, The Lion King became the highest grossing animated film of all time and held that title until 2003.

16) On the back wall of the back room of **Walt Disney: One Man's Dream** is a collage of pictures from Disney films. The Lion King is represented by a huge ensemble of characters from the film including Simba, Nala, Mufasa, Sarabi, Zazu, Rafiki, and a few more!

Once you have finished at Walt Disney: One Man's Dream, stop by **Sunset Boulevard** for your next references.

17) There is an advertisement for Fantasmic! in the windows of the connected stores **Sweet Spells** and **Villains In Vogue** on Sunset Boulevard. One of the characters shown in the advertisement is Scar.

18) You can also find Scar, among other Disney villains, on the walls inside the connected stores **Sweet Spells** and **Villains In Vogue**.

At the end of the day at Disney's Hollywood Studios, take in a show of **Fantasmic!** to find the remaining references within the park.

19) Once you enter the seating area for **Fantasmic!** take a look at the seating sections throughout the theatre. One of these seating sections is represented by a picture of Scar!

20) There is a scene during **Fantasmic!** that focuses on The Lion King. During this scene, Rafiki dances on the stage while various other animals dance on stage and on water floats. This scene continues on the water screen with Simba and Nala dancing to "I Just Can't Wait to be King." The scene transforms into the "Dancing Bubbles" segment of the show where you can see Simba, Timon, and Pumba walking across the log bridge as a very cool instrumental version of "Hakuna Matata" is played overhead.

21) Just after the Queen from Snow White calls upon the forces of evil in **Fantasmic!** Scar and other Disney villains appear on the water screen and can be found throughout the rest of the sequence with the villains.

22) You can find Rafiki on the steamboat at the very end of **Fantasmic!** along with several other Disney characters.

Fun Fact: The Lion King won two Academy Awards: one for Best Original Score and another for "Can You Feel the Love Tonight?" as Best Original Song.

Disney's Animal Kingdom

Once you arrive at Disney's Animal Kingdom, make your way to **Camp Minnie-Mickey** for the biggest reference to the film found throughout the Walt Disney World Resort.

23) The Lion King has been brought back to life in **The Festival of the Lion King**, one of the greatest stage shows in Disney. During the show, you can find Simba and Pumba, in audio-animatronic form, and Timon who acts as host. The show brings the songs from the film to life including "Circle of Life," "I Just Can't Wait to be King," "Can You Feel the Love Tonight?" and a few others with amazing twists, turns, and flips!

Stop by The Lion King's home country of **Africa** to hop on the train to **Rafiki's Planet Watch** which will take you to your next reference.

24) After arriving at **Rafiki's Planet Watch**, you will find several signs featuring Rafiki showing you the way (much like he did for Simba) to his Planet Watch Station. While there, look around for other sightings of Rafiki and his Lion King friends.

Fun Fact: Rafiki is the only Disney character, outside of Mickey and Minnie, to have an area of a park named after him. Not too bad for a baboon.

The final reference in Disney's Animal Kingdom can be found during **Mickey's Jammin' Jungle Parade**.

25) Rafiki can be found leading **Mickey's Jammin' Jungle Parade** on the first float where he takes the position of making sure things stay on task. You can also find Timon walking between floats during the parade.

Fun Fact: A lot of the names in The Lion King are Swahili words. Simba means "lion," Rafiki means "friend," and Hakuna Matata really does mean "no worries."

Downtown Disney

While in **Downtown Disney's Marketplace**, make sure you stop by **World of Disney** for the majority of the references in the area.

26) After entering **World of Disney** through the doors below Mickey and Minnie, you will be in a room with a high ceiling. Pay attention to the paintings of Mickey and the gang traveling around the world on the walls near the ceiling. One of the paintings is an African scene that has Simba, Nala, Rafiki, Scar, and a few other characters for the film present.

27) Look at the ceiling in the "Bird Room" in **World of Disney** to find a mural which features several birds including Zazu. He appears with co-manager of the Enchanted Tiki Room, Iago.

The final reference in **Downtown Disney** can be found while walking around **Downtown Disney's Marketplace**.

28) While strolling through **Downtown Disney's Marketplace**, listen for the song "Hakuna Matata." This is one of thirty-two songs that play in the area.

Resorts

The two resorts that feature references to The Lion King are **All-Star Movies** and **Pop Century**.

29) After entering the **World Premiere** food court in **All-Star Movies**, take a look at the wall on your left hand side to find one of the original posters for The Lion King.

30) The windows behind the bus stop at **All-Star Movies** feature several Disney characters including Simba!

31) While in the lobby of **Pop Century**, look in the shadow box dedicated to the animated films of the 1990's to find two Simba toys (one older, one younger) and a button of Mufasa and Simba together.

Fun Fact: The Lion King spawned a Broadway play of the same name, two films (The Lion King 2 and The Lion King 1 ½), and a television show starring Timon and Pumba.

"Pocahontas"

Released: June 23, 1995

The Film in Three Paragraphs

A crew of explorers set sail from England to the New World in hopes to find gold. The bravest of the crew, John Smith, talks about how he will take care of any savages in his way. Meanwhile in the New World, the audience is introduced to Pocahontas who is the daughter of the tribe's chief and goes wherever the wind takes her. When her father informs her of his plans to have her marry Kocoum, the great warrior of the tribe, she is far from excited.

Pocahontas visits with a weeping willow named Grandmother Willow. Pocahontas confides in her about a dream she has been having about a spinning arrow. Grandmother Willow tells Pocahontas to listen with her heart to the world around her. Following her advice, Pocahontas finds the ship John Smith is on. The two meet and quickly fall in love with one another. However, both Pocahontas' tribe and John Smith's crew feels threatened by each other and declare war.

One night, Kocoum sees Pocahontas and John Smith kissing. Out of jealousy, he attacks and is killed by a member of Smith's crew. The tribe takes John Smith into custody and plans to kill him the following morning. Pocahontas follows her heart and stops her father before he strikes John Smith. She declares her love for him, and the Chief decides to make peace with the newcomers. Governor Ratcliffe, the leader of the crew, aims his gun at the Chief and fires. However, John Smith jumps in the bullet's path and is hit instead. In the end, John Smith must return to London to receive proper medical treatment and the two star crossed lovers go their separate ways.

Magic Kingdom

The first Pocahontas reference you can find is on **Main Street, USA**.

1) In the back room of **Exposition Hall**, take a look at the Milestones in Disney Animation to find a "pencil sketch" of Pocahontas in the background. This sketch overlaps the Hercules and Hunchback of Notre Dame pictures.

The next reference can be found while riding the **Walt Disney World Railroad** between the Frontierland and Mickey's Toontown Fair stations.

2) While traveling between Frontierland and Mickey's Toontown Fair on the **Walt Disney World Railroad**, your host talks about how Pocahontas can be found "in these parts." Just after he says this, you can hear Pocahontas sing, "Colors of the Wind."

Fun Fact: Although not completely historically accurate, the animators did visit with Native American tribes to help make parts of the movie as historically accurate as possible.

Disney's Hollywood Studios

The first two references at Disney's Hollywood Studios can be found at the **Magic of Disney Animation** building in the **Animation Courtyard**.

3) While waiting in line for the **Magic of Disney Animation**, take a look at the concept art on the walls for various Disney films. One picture shows the meeting of Pocahontas and John Smith. I do not know if the animators could paint with all of the colors of the wind at this point in the production, but they definitely did during the final film. If you visit on a day when the entire line is not being used,

ask a cast member if you can take a look around. They are usually more than willing to let you.

4) During the **Magic of Disney Animation** show, you will learn about the different challenges animators must overcome while making a film. During this part of the show, you will learn about Pocahontas' sidekicks Meeko, Flit, and a potential third sidekick, a turkey. Obviously, adding a turkey would have made the movie a completely different experience and the animators finally settled on only Meeko and Flit.

Fantasmic! the nighttime show at Disney's Hollywood Studios, is home to the largest Pocahontas reference throughout Walt Disney World.

5) While walking on the path towards **Fantasmic!** look at the banners on either side of the path. One of these banners features Pocahontas. Once in the theatre, you can also sit in her section, which is represented by the same banner.

6) Pocahontas takes center stage during **Fantasmic!** One scene features John Smith, Governor Ratcliffe, the colonists, Chief Powhatan and his tribe, and, of course, Pocahontas in real life. In addition, Chief Powhatan, Grandmother Willow, Pocahontas, and John Smith appear on the water screen while "Colors of the Wind" plays in the background.

Fun Fact: In Disneyland's version of Fantasmic! which opened in 1992, the big battle scene focuses around Peter Pan. When Disney decided to have the popular show in Florida as well in 1998, they decided to use a modern film for the battle scene. Pocahontas, which was released a few years before, became the obvious choice.

7) At the end of **Fantasmic!** there is a group of Disney characters from various films on the steamboat with Mickey. Pocahontas, John Smith, and Meeko are present the majority of the time.

Fun Fact: Pocahontas premiered at New York's Central Park with 100,000 viewers giving it the honor of having the largest premiere of any Disney film.

Disney's Animal Kingdom

Fun Fact: Although there are no current references to Pocahontas in Disney's Animal Kingdom, there used to be a stage show called "Pocahontas and Her Forest Friends" in Camp Minnie-Mickey. The show focused around Pocahontas, Grandmother Willow, and live animals as they tried to figure out who the most resourceful animal was. In the end, we discovered it was us, humans!

Downtown Disney

The next group of references to Pocahontas can be found in **Downtown Disney's Marketplace**, mainly within the store **World of Disney**.

8) If you enter **World of Disney** through the doors below Mickey and Minnie, you will enter a room with a high ceiling. John Smith and Pocahontas are hanging high above you from the ceiling near the back portion of this room.

9) Stop by the "Bird Room" in **World of Disney** and look at the mural on the ceiling to find several animals in a tree. If you look at the corner of this picture, you will realize the tree is none other than Grandmother Willow. Flying close by is Flit!

10) Keep moving through the "Bird Room" of **World of Disney** until you reach the end of the store in "Princess Hall." In the back of this room is a stained glass window with pictures of different princesses' castles. Although Pocahontas does not have a castle, she is represented on the far left by pine trees, bushes, and a weeping willow.

11) While still in "Princess Hall" in **World of Disney**, head towards the exit of the store and look at the banner above the doors to find Pocahontas and seven other princesses on a sign which reads, "Happily Ever After."

12) As you stroll around **Downtown Disney's Marketplace**, listen for the song, "Colors of the Wind." This is one of thirty-two songs played in the area, so the odds of hearing it within the first few songs is pretty slim.

13) Just after entering **DisneyQuest**, but before boarding the elevators, take a look at the top of the pillars in the center of the room. One of the characters found here is Pocahontas.

Resorts

The final reference to the film can be found at **All-Star Movies**.

14) While waiting for the buses at **All-Star Movies**, look at the pictures inside the windows behind you to find Flit with several other Disney characters!

Fun Fact: The name Pocahontas means "little mischief."

"Toy Story"

Released: November 22, 1995

The Film in Three Paragraphs

Andy is downstairs opening presents with his friends at his birthday party while his toys, alive as can be, are upstairs listening through a baby monitor about the presents Andy is receiving. All of the toys are nervous that they will be replaced except Woody, a cowboy doll and Andy's current favorite toy. Andy, excited about a present his mom gave him, returns to his room, pushes Woody off of his honored spot on the bed, and places the new toy there.

The other toys are in shock that Woody is no longer on his spot, but he explains that it was just excitement and they should welcome the new toy. The new toy is a Buzz Lightyear Space Ranger, one of the coolest toys on the market. Buzz quickly begins to replace Woody as Andy's favorite toy. A few days later, Andy is told he can bring one toy to dinner with him. Woody plots to knock Buzz off the shelf they are on so Andy will pick him, but instead he knocks Buzz out the window. The other toys banish him from the room. Before they can do anything, Andy comes to take Woody to the restaurant.

On the way to the restaurant, Buzz shows up in the car. He and Woody begin to squabble and fall out of the car. The two are lost, but find their way to Pizza Planet, the restaurant Andy is going to for dinner. Unfortunately, Sid, Andy's toy destroying next door neighbor, finds them first and brings them home with him. Fearing the worse, Woody desperately tries to escape, but Buzz, finally realizing he is just a toy and not a space ranger, is no help. Woody convinces Buzz that being a toy is a lot cooler than being a space ranger. The two end up escaping and become the best of friends.

Magic Kingdom

Your first two references can be found on **Main Street, USA**.

1) If you go to the backroom of **Exposition Hall,** you will find the Milestones of Disney Animation on the back wall. One of the pictures shown is Sheriff Woody tilting his hat. Underneath the picture is a sign explaining why this film is considered a milestone in Disney animation.

2) You can take a picture of yourself in a scene from different Disney films in the backroom of **Exposition Hall**. One

scene is the crane machine in Toy Story. You can put your head inside a green alien's head and have your picture with the green aliens and their master, "The Claw."

Your next reference is located in Mickey's Country House at **Mickey's Toontown Fair**.

3) Have you ever wondered what Buzz Lightyear's return address was before joining Andy's room? Just after entering **Mickey's Country House**, take a look at the front table to find Mickey's mail. A letter from Buzz Lightyear shows he is from "Infinity and Beyond." You can also find a letter from Woody that has the return address of "Andy's Room."

Your final group of references in the Magic Kingdom can be found in **Tomorrowland**.

4) "Attention Space Rangers! Buzz Lightyear needs your help!" Have you ever wanted to save the universe from the Evil Emperor Zurg? Now you can! Grab your blaster and make your way to **Buzz Lightyear's Space Ranger Spin**. While in line for the ride, Buzz will give you your mission. Throughout the ride you can find the little green aliens from the film and Buzz Lightyear himself.

5) After exiting Buzz Lightyear's Space Ranger Spin, leave the building and make your way to the outdoor **gift shop**, which is near the Tomorrowland Transit Authority entrance. The Little Green Aliens have taken residency in their spaceship on the top of the stand.

6) While riding the **Tomorrowland Transit Authority**, you may get your call to help defend the galaxy from Buzz Lightyear himself. You can also see part of Buzz Lightyear's Space Ranger Spin during the ride.

7) **Character Meet and Greet Alert!** Just after exiting **Buzz Lightyear's Space Ranger Spin**, head to your right to find the area where you can meet Buzz Lightyear himself!

8) While walking around **Tomorrowland**, you may hear an instrumental version of the song "Strange Things" playing from time to time.

Fun Fact: The voice of Hamm the piggy bank, John Ratzenberger, is considered a Pixar good luck charm and has gone on to provide a voice a character in each Pixar full length feature film.

Epcot

The only reference to Toy Story can be found in **World Showcase**.

9) **Character Meet and Greet Alert!** You can meet Woody and Buzz Lightyear at various times at **The American Adventure** pavilion.

Fun Fact: The film's popularity actually led to the creation of two sequels, Toy Story 2 in 1999 and Toy Story 3 which has a scheduled release in 2010. For references to Toy Story 2, please refer to its own individual chapter within this book.

Disney's Hollywood Studios

The first reference to Toy Story in Disney's Hollywood Studios is near the **Streets of America**.

10) While facing Muppet Vision 3-D, look to your left for one of the best film oriented restaurants in all of Walt Disney World, **Toy Story Pizza Planet**. You can find several references to Toy Story in and around this pizza joint. On the outside of the building is Woody and Buzz on the higher

roof, while Mr. Potato Head hangs out by the Pizza Planet sign. If you are looking for Slinky, he is on the roof above the Fish Co. sign.

11) Inside **Toy Story Pizza Planet** are murals depicting the green aliens with additional green aliens hanging from the ceiling in the dining area. You can find the game "Whack-A-Alien" that Sid played in the film in the game area. Behind the game, you can find Buzz and Woody with very shocked looks upon their faces.

After finishing your pizza, make your way over to **Pixar Place** for your next reference.

12) Please note that since **Toy Story Midway Mania** focuses around both Toy Story and Toy Story 2, the entire list of references for the attraction are in the Toy Story 2 chapter of this book.

After Toy Story Midway Mania, stop by the **Animation Courtyard** for your next group of references.

13) While in line for the **Magic of Disney Animation**, you can find a piece of concept art that features Sid on one of the walls. He appears to look more like a teenager than a child, but he still keeps his role as toy torturer. If you visit on a day when the entire line is not being used, ask a cast member if you can take a look around. They are typically more than willing to let you.

14) You can find a small Rex toy on the top desk shelf behind the drawing of Mushu in the room where the main show for the **Magic of Disney Animation** takes place.

15) When your host discusses how everyone has their own favorite Disney character at the beginning of the **Magic of Disney Animation** show, watch the screen closely. One of the characters that appears quickly on the screen is Buzz Lightyear.

16) Is your personality similar to Buzz Lightyear's? You can find out at the **You're a Character** game in the **Magic of Disney Animation** building. Please note that if your goal is to have Buzz as your result, try to answer the questions as you believe he would.

Fun Fact: Unlike previous Disney films, only 110 animators worked on the film instead of the more typical 500 plus animators.

The final reference in Disney's Hollywood studios can be found during the afternoon parade, **Block Party Bash**.

17) The majority of the characters from the film can be found on the toy blocks on the first float during the **Block Party Bash**. Throughout the Block Party Bash, the Green Army Men set the party mood by being your host for each section of the parade. You can also see Mr. Potato Head, Woody, Buzz, Lenny, and Bo Peep dancing on the street just a few feet away from you. Take note, if you sit close to the curb you may actually be one of the lucky people to be invited onto the street to dance with the characters.

Fun Fact: Buzz Lightyear got his name from astronaut Buzz Aldrin.

Downtown Disney

Your first stop at Downtown Disney is at the store **Once Upon a Toy**.

18) The main entrance of **Once Upon a Toy** provides the perfect photo opportunity with a life-size statue of Buzz Lightyear and Mr. Potato Head.

19) Just after entering the first room in **Once Upon a Toy**, look up at the ceiling to find Sheriff Woody in the rafters.

20) There is a mural behind the cash register in the center room of **Once Upon a Toy**. If you look closely, you may be able to find Woody, Buzz, Mr. Potato Head, and Rex hidden within the painting.

21) While walking around **Downtown Disney's Marketplace**, listen for the song "You've Got a Friend in Me" from the film. This is one of thirty-two songs played in the area, so the odds of hearing it within the first few songs are pretty slim.

Your next stop is **Downtown Disney's Westside**.

22) Look up in **Planet Hollywood's** main dining area to find Sherriff Woody looking down at you.

23) You can become a space ranger in a new twist on bumper cars at **Buzz Lightyear's Astroblasters** in **DisneyQuest**. Buzz adorns the sign for the ride and is on the height check sign.

24) **DisneyQuest** is also home to **Sid's Create-a-Toy**, an interactive computer game that allows you to make your own mixed up toys.

25) Just after entering **DisneyQuest**, but before boarding the elevators, take a look at the top of the pillars in the center of the room. One of the characters found here is Buzz Lightyear.

Fun Fact: With Toy Story's success, a few references from the film began appearing in future Pixar films. For instance, the Pizza Planet truck can be found in every Pixar film since Toy Story's release.

Resorts

The first resort you can find references at is **All-Star Movies**.

26) My all time favorite Disney resort is **All-Star Movies** due to the fact that you are surrounded by classic Disney films at all times, both in the parks and at your resort. The resort hosts the largest reference to Toy Story throughout all of Walt Disney World. How big? Three stories big! The largest Woody and Buzz Lightyear toys are the center pieces of the Toy Story area. You can also find what is probably the largest door in all of Walt Disney World, which is appropriately marked, "Andy's Room." Take a look at the clouds on each level representing the wallpaper in Andy's room. You can also find the toy soldiers at the top of the buildings and a large Bo Peep, Rex, and R.C. in the area.

The final reference to Toy Story found throughout all of Walt Disney World is at **Pop Century**.

27) While at **Pop Century**, take a look at the shadow boxes in the lobby. Inside the shadow box that shows animated films from the 1990's are small toy figurines of Buzz, Woody, and Rex.

Fun Fact: Before Toy Story, Pixar focused on short films, much like the Disney Company did before Snow White. Prior to Toy Story, Pixar had released five short films including Tin Toy, a story about a toy, which caught Disney's attention and caused the two companies to join forces.

"The Hunchback of Notre Dame"

Released: June 21, 1996

The Film in Three Paragraphs

The film begins with Judge Claude Frollo killing a gypsy woman because he believes she is in possession of stolen goods.

When he realizes that it was actually a baby who looks like a monster, he decides to throw the child down a well. Just before he kills the child, the Archdeacon stops him and convinces him to raise the child as his own. Frollo agrees and keeps the child in the bell tower of Notre Dame. The child grows up to be a hunchback named Quasimodo.

When Quasimodo sneaks down to the Festival of Fools, he is named the ugliest person in all of Paris, which is actually an honor. Unfortunately, things take a turn for the worse and the crowd starts to pelt him with tomatoes, eggs, and other items. Luckily, a beautiful gypsy named Esmeralda comes to Quasimodo's rescue and escapes with him into Notre Dame where she claims sanctuary. Frollo posts guards at every door to prevent her escape, but she sneaks out with assistance from Quasimodo and invites him to join her some day in her hideout.

Frollo becomes obsessed with trying to find Esmeralda and begins to burn down all of Paris. This causes the Captain of the Guard, Phoebus, to object to Frollo's plans. Upset by Phoebus' defiance, Frollo makes Phoebus an outcast as well. When Frollo announces that he has learned the location of the Court of Miracles, the gypsy's hideout, Quasimodo and Phoebus set out to warn Esmeralda and the gypsies. Frollo follows them, captures Esmeralda, and the following day prepares to burn her at the stake. Quasimodo saves Esmeralda and eventually defeats Frollo. In the end, Phoebus and Esmeralda become a couple, and Quasimodo is finally accepted by society.

Magic Kingdom

Your first reference to the film can be found on **Main Street, USA**.

1) There is a picture of Laverne with Quasimodo in the Milestones in Disney Animation mural, which is located in the back room of **Exposition Hall**.

The only other reference at the Magic Kingdom is during the show **Dream Along with Mickey**, which is performed on the stage in front of the castle.

2) During **Dream Along with Mickey**, listen to the music when Maleficent takes center stage. The music is from the Hunchback of Notre Dame.

Fun Fact: Achilles, Phoebus' horse, was given his name by the production team so Phoebus could simply make the joke, "Achilles, heel."

Epcot

The only references in Epcot to The Hunchback of Notre Dame can be found in **World Showcase**.

3) In the back room of **Plume et Palette** in the **France** pavilion is a book that has a brief recap of the film. In addition to that, you can find a book on a shelf which is entitled "Notre Dame de Paris".

4) **Character Meet and Greet Alert!** Occasionally you can find characters from the film, usually Clopin and Quasimodo, doing meet and greets around **France**. Please note this is becoming a very rare opportunity, so double check with a cast member to see if these characters are doing meet and greets during your visit.

Disney's Hollywood Studios

The first group of references at Disney's Hollywood Studios can be found in the **Animation Courtyard**.

5) While waiting in line for the **Magic of Disney Animation**, you can find a piece of concept art that shows Quasimodo showing off his strength by hoisting a pillar above his

head. Frollo's face can be found on another sketch where he wears a truly evil face. If you visit on a day when the entire line is not being used, ask if you can take a look around. The cast members are usually more than willing to help you out.

6) While in the room where the opening show for the **Magic of Disney Animation** takes place you can find a Quasimodo doll on a shelf on the left hand side of the room.

7) During the **Magic of Disney Animation** show, your host discusses how they bring characters movements to life. During this part of the film, a clip of Phoebus showing off his sword handling skills is shown.

8) As you stroll around the **Animation Courtyard**, keep your ears open for the song "Topsy, Turvy Day," which is one of the songs that plays in the area.

Fun Fact: Mary Wickes, the actress who provided the voice of Laverne, passed away while the film was still in production. She had worked with Disney in the Annette television show, which ran on the Mickey Mouse Club from 1957-1958, and in the 1972 film Snowball Express.

Your final reference in Disney's Hollywood Studios can be found during **Fantasmic!**

9) Just after the Queen from Snow White transforms into the Hag in **Fantasmic!** she calls upon all the forces of evil. In response to her call, Judge Claude Frollo appears on the water screen and can be found throughout the rest of the sequence with other Disney villains.

Fun Fact: The Hunchback of Notre Dame had a stage show of the same name in the Streets of America section of Disney's Hollywood Studios until 2002.

Downtown Disney

The first stop at Downtown Disney is **Disney's Days of Christmas** shop.

10) **Disney's Days of Christmas** has created its own version of the classic song, "12 Days of Christmas." You can find different Disney characters representing each day in and outside of the store. The fourth day of Christmas focuses around bells and our favorite bell ringer, Quasimodo.

11) If you enter **World of Disney** through the entrance that is below Mickey and Minnie, you can find scenes of Mickey and the gang traveling around the world on the walls near the ceiling. One of the locations they visit is Notre Dame where they meet with Quasimodo, Laverne, Victor, and Hugo.

Resorts

The final reference to the film can be found at **All-Star Movies**.

12) While waiting for the buses at **All-Star Movies,** take a look at the pictures in the windows on the wall behind you to find Esmeralda among several other Disney characters. You can also find a film canister in the picture which reads, "Hunchback '96.'"

Fun Fact: Victor and Hugo, two of the gargoyles in the film, were named after the author of "The Hunchback of Notre Dame," Victor Hugo.

"Hercules"

Released: June 27, 1997

The Film in Three Paragraphs

Hades, god of the underworld, plans to attack and conquer Mount Olympus in eighteen years when the planets align and release his henchmen, the Titans. However, Hades learns that if Hercules, son of Zeus, joins the fight against him, his attack will fail. To remove this threat, Hades decides to make Hercules mortal and then kill him. Just before his two henchmen, Pain and Panic, kill Hercules, a couple finds the baby Hercules and decide to adopt him.

Almost eighteen years pass and Hercules is considered an outcast since he is unable to control his strength. His parents tell him that they found him with the symbol of the gods around his neck. Hercules goes to the temple of Zeus to investigate and discovers that his father is Zeus and he is also supposed to be a god. Zeus explains that in order to join him, Hercules must become a hero and sends him to a satyr named Philoctetes, or Phil for short, for guidance. Phil is reluctant at first, but takes Hercules under his wing. After completing his training, Hercules saves a beautiful girl named Meg and instantly becomes enamored with her. Meg, however, is secretly working for Hades and leads Hercules to what should be instant danger. Instead, Hercules saves the day and becomes the most popular person in Thebes.

Hades finally realizes that he should send Meg to find Hercules' weak spot and soon discovers that Hercules would do anything to keep Meg safe. Hades makes a deal not to hurt Meg if Hercules forfeits his strength while Hades attacks Mount Olympus. Hercules agrees and Hades begins to conquer Mount Olympus. During the attack, Meg is injured; Hercules regains his strength, saves Mount Olympus, but, when he returns to Meg, he finds that she has passed on. He makes one final deal with Hades that if he saves Meg from the underworld, Hades must release her. Hades agrees and Hercules rescues Meg. By attempting the daring rescue that forced him to risk his own life, he proves himself to be a true hero and becomes a god. In the end, Hercules decides he would rather stay mortal on earth with Meg than be immortal without her.

Magic Kingdom

The first reference to Hercules can be found on **Main Street, USA**.

1) The Milestones in Disney Animation, which can be found in the back room of **Exposition Hall**, features a picture of Hercules looking as mighty as ever.

Walk to the end of Main Street, USA and go through the castle into **Fantasyland** for your next reference.

2) While waiting in line for **Mickey's Philharmagic**, you can find posters of upcoming attractions including one with the fiery villain Hades who sings "Torch Songs."

The final reference in the Magic Kingdom can be found during **Wishes**, the nighttime fireworks show.

3) One of the scenes in **Wishes** focuses around an instrumental version of "Go the Distance."

Fun Fact: Ron Clements and John Musker, the directors of the film, decided to give the film a more hip edge to help viewers look at a subject that some found dull as entertaining.

Disney's Hollywood Studios

The first group of references in Disney's Hollywood Studios can be found in the **Animation Courtyard**.

4)   While waiting in line for the **Magic of Disney Animation,** take a look at the concept sketches on the walls. I won't say I'm in love with this picture, but there is a picture showing Hercules and Meg on their day off. If you visit on a day when the entire line is not being used, ask a cast member if you can take a look around. They are typically more than willing to oblige.

5)   At the beginning of the **Magic of Disney Animation** show, your host discusses how everyone has their own favorite Disney character. During this introduction, watch the screen to see various Disney animated characters from different films including Hercules himself.

For your next reference, make your way over to **Sunset Boulevard**.

6)   If you take a look in one of the windows of the connected stores **Sweet Spells** and **Villains In Vogue,** you can find Hades and his villainous friends in an advertisement for the nighttime show, Fantasmic!

The remaining references in Disney's Hollywood Studios can be found during the nighttime show **Fantasmic!**

7)   There are banners on both sides of the walkway that lead into the theatre for **Fantasmic!** including a banner of Hades. The same banner can be found inside the theatre marking the Hades seating section.

8)   During the **Dancing Bubbles** sequence of **Fantasmic!** keep your eyes open for Hercules, Phil, the Muses, and Pegasus. They are all in their own bubbles while an instrumental version of the song "Zero to Hero" plays overhead.

9)   After Mickey rubs a magic lamp in **Fantasmic!** the villains gain power and several villains, including Hades, appear on the water screen.

10) Several Disney characters from various films are on the steamboat with Mickey at the very end of **Fantasmic!** Meg and Hercules are present at times, but are not guaranteed to be there every show.

Fun Fact: Andreas Deja, who had previously animated characters like Jafar, Gaston, and Scar, finally animated a protagonist in a film by animating Hercules.

Downtown Disney

11) While walking around **Downtown Disney's Marketplace**, listen for the song "One Last Hope" from Hercules. This is one of thirty-two songs that is played in the area, so the odds of hearing it within the first few songs are pretty slim. You can also hear this song in **World of Disney** from time to time.

Fun Fact: During the film, Pain and Panic become stuck under a boulder when they are disguised like children and exclaim, "Somebody call IX-I-I!" IX-I-I are the Roman Numerals for 9-1-1.

Resorts

The only resorts that hold references to Hercules are **All-Star Movies** and **Pop Century**.

12) While waiting for the buses at **All-Star Movies**, look into the windows of the shop **Donald's Double Features** to find a mural of several Disney characters including Hercules! In addition to finding Hercules in this picture, you can also find a film canister labeled, "Hercules '97."

13) There is a shadow box that focuses on Disney Animation in the 1990's in the lobby of **Pop Century**. In the shadow

box is a Hercules toy that came out around the time of the film's release.

Fun Fact: The film was originally going to have its premiere in Greece. However, too many people were upset by the changes Disney had made to the film from the original story that permission was not granted.

"Mulan"

Released: June 19, 1998

The Film in Three Paragraphs

When the Huns invade China, the Emperor orders that one man from each family must join the army. To protect her father, Mulan steals her father's sword and armor, cuts her hair, and joins the army in his place. The family ancestors, realizing that they must save and protect Mulan, argue over which guardian they should send after her. They finally agree on the Great Stone Dragon and send Mushu, the gong ringer, to wake him. In the process, however, Mushu destroys the Great Stone Dragon. Instead of informing the ancestors, he decides to chase Mulan down and be her guardian.

Mushu catches up to Mulan and begins coaching her on how to be a man. When they arrive at the solider camp, Mulan, now going by the name Ping, makes a bad impression with everyone immediately thanks to Mushu's tips. When training begins, Mulan is typically at the bottom of the pack until she begins to use her brain instead of her physical strength. After her change in strategy, she becomes the top student in the group. When Mushu thinks Mulan is ready to go to war, he creates a letter stating that another division of the army needs their help and delivers it to Chi-Fu, a member of the Emperor's council who is working with Mulan's division.

When the soldiers arrive at the battle scene, they realize the previous division lost the battle. They then encounter Shan Yu, the leader of the Huns. Thanks to Mulan's cleverness, she causes an avalanche, which in turn defeats the entire Hun army. In the process, she is wounded. After receiving medical attention, the doctor realizes she is a woman and she becomes an outcast by her fellow soldiers. After the army leaves, Shan Yu and a few of his warriors emerge from the snow. Mulan sees this and chases them to the Emperor's palace. In the end, Mulan stops Shan Yu from killing the Emperor, and the Emperor gives Mulan and her family highest honors for the sacrifices Mulan made for her country and saving the Emperor's life.

Magic Kingdom

The first reference for Mulan can be found on **Main Street, USA**.

1) Stop by **Exposition Hall** and look at the Milestones in Disney animation in the back room to find a picture of a stunned Mushu.

The only remaining reference to Mulan in the Magic Kingdom is during the **Celebrate A Dream Come True Parade**.

2) During the **Celebrate A Dream Come True Parade**, pay close attention to Peter Pan's float. Behind Peter Pan is a hard to see "merry-go-round," which contains Mushu as one of the characters going around in circles.

Fun Fact: The flags that are present throughout the majority of the film were inspired by the flags the producer saw on the Great Wall of China while visiting China in preparation of the film.

Epcot

The only reference to Mulan found throughout Epcot is in **World Showcase**.

3) **Character Meet and Greet Alert!** You can meet Mulan and Mushu in the **China** pavilion at various times throughout the day.

Fun Fact: Christina Aguilera filmed her music video for the song "Reflection" at the China Pavilion in Epcot.

Disney's Hollywood Studios

Your first group of references in Disney's Hollywood Studios can be found in the **Animation Courtyard**.

4) While waiting in line for the **Magic of Disney Animation**, you can find concept sketches on the walls for different Disney films including one that shows Mulan dressed up as Ping. If this area of the line is not being used, ask a cast member if you can take a look around. They are usually more than willing to let you.

5) The **Magic of Disney Animation** show revolves around Mushu as he discovers how he came into existence. If you are a Mushu fan, this is a must see!

6) There are drawings that were used for the film on the left hand side of the room where the **Magic of Disney Animation** show takes place. You can also find a drawing of Mushu on the sketch board behind the host.

7) Is your personality similar to Mushu's? You can find out on the **You're a Character** game in the **Magic of Disney Animation**. Please note that you may not always get Mushu, or ever get him, but if your goal is to have Mushu as your result, try to answer the questions as you believe he would.

8) In the waiting area for the **Animation Academy** inside the **Magic of Disney Animation** building is a large pencil sketch of Mulan on the wall.

9) There is an ensemble of pictures from Disney films on one of the back walls at **Walt Disney: One Man's Dream**. One of the films represented is Mulan with a picture of Mulan sitting with her father, Fa Zhou.

Fun Fact: The Disney Stars and Motor Cars Parade, which ran from 2001 until 2008, had a float that featured Mulan and Mushu.

Your final references at Disney's Hollywood Studios can be found during the nighttime show **Fantasmic!**

10) During the "Dancing Bubbles" sequence of **Fantasmic!** you can hear an instrumental version of "I'll Make a Man Out of You" playing while Cri-kee, Mulan, and Mushu dance in their own bubbles on the water screen.

11) At the end of **Fantasmic!** you can find several characters on the steamboat with Mickey. Mulan and Mushu are present the majority of the time, but are not guaranteed to be there for every show.

Fun Fact: Near the end of the film, Mushu ambushes two men working at the palace. The two men in this scene are actually caricatures of the two directors of the film.

Downtown Disney

The two references to Mulan in Downtown Disney can be found at **Downtown Disney's Marketplace**.

12) Above the exit in "Princess Hall" within **World of Disney** is a huge banner which reads, "Happily Ever After." On this sign you will find Mulan with seven other Disney princesses.

13) While walking around **Downtown Disney's Marketplace**, listen for the song "I'll Make a Man Out of You." This is one of thirty-two songs played in the area.

Resorts

The final reference to the film found throughout Walt Disney World is located at **All-Star Movies**.

14) Just after exiting **Donald's Double Feature** towards the buses at **All-Star Movies**, take a look into the windows to find Cri-kee and Mushu!

Fun Fact: Mulan's horse, Khan, was actually named after one of the writer's dogs.

"a bug's life"

Released: November 20, 1998

The Film in Three Paragraphs

Each year a colony of ants prepares food for a colony of grasshoppers that in return provide the ants protection. When an ant named Flik accidentally knocks the food offering off a cliff and into the water below, the grasshoppers give them one last chance to make their annual payment. Flik suggests to Princess Atta, an ant training to be queen, that they send someone to get warrior bugs to help the colony out. She decides it would be better to have Flik out of the way so he does not screw things up and sends him on his way.

Meanwhile near the "big city," a group of circus bugs get fired from their job. When Flik comes across the group, he finds them fighting a few flies and instantly believes they are warrior bugs. He offers them the job, and the circus bugs, thinking they have a performance, agree. Once they arrive at the colony, the circus bugs realize they are supposed to fight the grasshoppers and try to back out. Flik comes up with an idea to make a bird to scare off the grasshoppers. The circus bugs agree to go along with the plan and pretend like it is their own.

Eventually, the colony of ants realizes the warriors are simply circus bugs and send them and Flik away from the colony. Just after they leave, the grasshoppers arrive and threaten the Queen's life. The Queen's youngest daughter, Dot, escapes and warns Flik. Flik returns and begins to use the bird plan, but it fails. Hopper, leader of the grasshoppers, takes Flik away, and they eventually arrive in front of a bird's nest. Hopper, believing the bird to be another fake, taunts it and is eventually eaten by the bird's chicks. In the end, the colony is safe and they welcome Flik back with open arms, I mean legs.

Magic Kingdom

Your journey begins on **Main Street, USA**.

1) In the back room of **Exposition Hall** is a picture of everyone's favorite "warrior bugs" on the Milestones in Disney Animation mural on the back wall.

Fun Fact: P.T. Flea's name was inspired by well known circus man P.T. Barnum.

Disney's Hollywood Studios

Your first group of references in Disney's Hollywood Studios can be found in the **Animation Courtyard**.

2) At the beginning of the **Magic of Disney Animation** show, watch the screen as your host talks about how everyone has their own favorite Disney character. If you watch closely, you may be able to find Flik by himself and a different shot of Flik with Francis and Heimlich.

3) Is your personality similar to Princess Dot or Flik? You can find out by playing the **You're a Character** game in the **Magic of Disney Animation** building. Please take note that you may not always get either of these characters, or ever get them, but if your goal is to have Dot or Flik as your result, try to answer the questions as you believe they would.

4) In the back room of **Walt Disney: One Man's Dream** is an ensemble of pictures on the back wall including one of the circus turned warrior bugs.

Fun Fact: Disney's California Adventure in California has an entire section of the park devoted to "a bug's life," which is appropriately called "a bug's land."

Your final reference at Disney's Hollywood Studios can be found during the **Block Party Bash**.

5) One of the floats in **Block Party Bash** features the majority of the characters from the film. In addition to the characters, you can see the circus bugs' car, which is made out of a Casey Jr. Cookies box.

Fun Fact: The trailer near the bug city is also used in Monsters, Inc. when Randall, the villain of the film, meets his doom.

Disney's Animal Kingdom

The first three references to "a bug's life" in Disney's Animal Kingdom are on **Discovery Island**.

6) If you love 3-D films and a bug's life, then **"it's tough to be a bug"** is the best show for you. Within the Tree of Life, Flik shows the audience what it is like to be a bug by making them "honorary bugs." There is a scary encounter with Hopper

during the show so please take note that some children who love the film may be scared by portions of this show.

Fun Fact: "it's tough to be a bug" marks the second time in Disney history when an attraction was released before the animated film. The attraction opened with the park on April 22, 1998, seven months before the film was released.

7) **Character Meet and Greet Alert!** You can meet Flik and Princess Atta at various times throughout the day on the **Discovery Island Trails** just across the path from Pizza-fari.

8) A statue of Princess Atta is the center piece of **Creature Comforts**.

The final reference in the park is located at **Rafiki's Planet Watch**.

8) While in the **Conservation Station**, take a look at the back wall of the farthest room on the left to find a poster that discusses the "Super-heroes of the animal world," and features Flik!

Fun Fact: John Ratzenberger, who provides a voice in each feature length Pixar film, was the voice of P.T. Flea in a bug's life.

"Tarzan"

Released: June 18, 1999

The Film in Three Paragraphs

A couple with a young baby are shipwrecked and take up residence in a self-built tree house on a tropical island. The parents are killed by a leopard and the baby is abandoned in the family's tree house. Meanwhile in the jungle, two gorillas have lost their child and are having a tough time getting over their loss. When Kala, the mother gorilla, comes across the abandoned human infant, she takes him as her own and names him Tarzan. Tarzan is accepted by many gorillas, but is looked down on by Kala's husband and leader of the gorillas, Kerchak. Tarzan vows that he will be the best gorilla ever to prove himself to Kerchak.

Tarzan eventually grows up and mimics all the different animals within the jungle. Sabor, the leopard that killed Tarzan's parents, arrives at the gorilla camp and duels Tarzan. Tarzan prevails and is finally accepted by everyone within the gorilla family, except Kerchak. Almost as soon as the battle is over, the gorillas hear a gun shot and Tarzan goes to investigate. Tarzan finds a damsel in distress named Jane and saves her from a herd of monkeys. Jane introduces Tarzan to her father, Professor Archimedes Q. Porter, and their guide, Clayton. Clayton tries to convince Tarzan to show them where the gorillas live, but Jane takes control and begins teaching Tarzan all about the world.

Jane and Tarzan quickly fall in love with one another. When Jane's ship arrives to take her back to England, Tarzan decides that if he shows her the gorillas, she will stay with him. Once they arrive at the gorilla's nesting grounds, Clayton marks off where to find the gorillas. They leave the gorillas and head towards the ship. Clayton then detains the three humans and heads back to capture all of the gorillas. Tarzan escapes and faces Clayton in one final battle. In the end, Clayton gets caught up in some vines, Kerchak is shot, but the rest of the gorillas are safe. Tarzan becomes the new leader of the gorillas and must stay in the jungle to watch over his family. At the last minute, Jane and Porter decide to stay behind and live in the jungle with Tarzan and his gorilla family.

Magic Kingdom

The first reference to Tarzan found throughout Walt Disney World is located on **Main Street, USA.**

1) There is a picture of Tarzan "skating" down a tree in the Milestones in Disney Animation mural on the back wall of the back room in **Exposition Hall**. If you look underneath the picture, you can read why Tarzan is considered a milestone in Disney animation.

Fun Fact: When riding the Jungle Cruise, you will discover a camp overrun by gorillas. Look familiar? It should! The "Trashing the Camp" scene from the film was inspired by this part of the Jungle Cruise.

Disney's Hollywood Studios

All of your references found within Disney's Hollywood Studios are found in the **Animation Courtyard** area of the park.

2) While your host discusses that everyone has their own favorite Disney character at the beginning of the **Magic of Disney Animation** show, you can find a picture of young Tarzan on the screen.

3) There is a playground styled game that allows you to mix and match body parts of different characters while waiting in line to meet characters in the **Magic of Disney Animation**. One of the characters found here is the often overlooked Jane.

4) If you make your way to the back room of **Walt Disney: One Man's Dream**, take a look at the back wall to find an ensemble of pictures. One of the pictures included is from Tarzan.

Fun Fact: While riding the Great Movie Ride, you can see an earlier live action film version of Tarzan, 1932's Tarzan the Ape Man.

Disney's Animal Kingdom

The only reference to the film in Disney's Animal Kingdom can be found during **Mickey's Jammin' Jungle Parade**.

5) Terk is one of the characters walking in between the floats during **Mickey's Jammin' Jungle Parade**.

Fun Fact: There use to be an amazing acrobatic show that revolved around the film entitled **Tarzan Rocks**, but it unfortunately closed in January of 2006. The show took place in the Theatre in the Wild, which is now home to Finding Nemo: The Musical.

Downtown Disney

The final reference to Tarzan can be found while walking around **Downtown Disney's Marketplace**.

6) While walking through **Downtown Disney's Marketplace**, listen for the song "You'll Be in My Heart" from the film. This is one of thirty-two songs that play in the area, so the odds of hearing it within the first few songs are pretty slim.

Fun Fact: Glen Keane, the supervising animator for Tarzan himself, was inspired by his child's skateboarding skills to make Tarzan look as if he were skating through the trees.

"Toy Story 2"

Released: November 24, 1999

The Film in Three Paragraphs

When Woody's arm gets ripped, Andy is forced to leave him at home while he attends cowboy camp. After Andy leaves, one of his toys is placed in a garage sale. Woody ends up rescuing him, but is left behind in the process. A greedy toy collector by the name of Al finds Woody at the sale and steals him. Buzz and the other toys quickly discover that Al is actually the owner of Al's Toy Barn, a local toy store, and set off to rescue Woody.

When Woody arrives at Al's apartment, he meets Jessie, Bullseye, and Stinky Pete, all of whom complete the Roundup Gang from the hit television show "Woody's Roundup." Woody realizes that he was a star, but is disheartened when he learns that Al plans to sell the group, and other collectibles from the show, to a museum exhibit in Japan. Stinky Pete begins to convince Woody that being behind glass is better than being with Andy since Andy will grow up and forget him. On the other hand, Woody will bring joy daily to children in Japan.

Buzz and the gang arrive to rescue Woody, but he refuses to return home with them. As his friends begin to leave, Woody realizes that he would not miss Andy growing up for anything and invites the Roundup Gang to join him. Jessie and Bullseye accept the invitation, but Stinky Pete locks them in the room to prevent their escape. Buzz and the rest of Andy's toys chase Al, who has Woody and the Roundup Gang with him, to the airport. They eventually rescue Woody, Bullseye, and Jessie and attach Stinky Pete to a girl's backpack. When Andy returns home, he is thrilled to find the new toys and fixes Woody's arm making him much buffer.

Magic Kingdom

Your first reference can be found while in **Fantasyland**.

1) The line for **Mickey's Philharmagic** has posters that advertise past and upcoming attractions. One of the posters features Wheezy and reads, "An Evening with Wheezy: Now in its Final Squeak!"

The remaining reference in the Magic Kingdom is found in **Tomorrowland**.

2) You can find Buzz Lightyear and his archenemy, the evil Emperor Zurg throughout **Buzz Lightyear's Space Ranger Spin**. The goal of the ride is to shoot at the Z's found throughout the ride, which are in the same design as the Z's used on Zurg's toy box in the film.

Fun Fact: The short cartoon that was re-released with the film, 1986's "Luxo Jr.," was the cartoon that inspired Pixar's bouncing lamp logo.

Epcot

The only reference found throughout Epcot can be found in **World Showcase**.

3) **Character Meet and Greet Alert!** You can meet Woody, Buzz, Jessie, and Bullseye for a photo opportunity in **The American Adventure** pavilion. Please note that these characters are not available every day so ask a cast member when the best time to find them would be.

Fun Fact: Pixar originally planned to have Barbie make an appearance in the first Toy Story film; however, Disney and Pixar were unable to attain permission. After the success of Toy Story, they were granted permission to use Barbie in the sequel.

Disney's Hollywood Studios

Your first stop in the park is at the newest land, **Pixar Place**.

4) **Character Meet and Greet Alert!** Visit the Character Meet and Greet area across from the entrance to **Toy Story Midway Mania** in **Pixar Place** for a chance to meet Woody and Buzz.

5) Pixar Place is home to one of the greatest new attractions found throughout Walt Disney World, **Toy Story Midway Mania**. Outside the entrance by the roof is a formation of toy soldiers and a barrel of monkeys. Also, look at the scrabble board, which spells out the song title, "You've Got a Friend in Me."

6) While in line for **Toy Story Midway Mania**, you can find Andy's drawings on the walls including the Mr. Potato Head "wanted poster" and the cows drawn on cardboard boxes from the first film. You can also find some drawings of Buzz.

7) Mr. Potato Head greets the guests who are waiting in line for **Toy Story Midway Mania**. Mr. Potato Head actually interacts with the crowd and at times calls people who are standing in line to answer questions. The standby line provides the best viewing for this reference.

8) As you start **Toy Story Midway Mania**, you will pass under a sign with Woody and Jessie. The first game, Hamm and Eggs, consists of throwing eggs and is hosted by everyone's favorite piggybank, Hamm. Bo Peep's Baaaloon Pop focuses around Bo Peep and her sheep. The Green Army Men host the game Green Army Men Shoot Camp, a baseball throwing game. Buzz Lightyear's Fling Tossers is a ring toss game hosted by Buzz and Woody's Rootin' Tootin' Shootin' Gallery is hosted by everyone's favorite sheriff.

9) Just before entering or exiting the ride vehicles for **Toy Story Midway Mania**, take a look at the side of the vehicle. Notice how each ride vehicle features a different character from both Toy Story films.

The next reference is in the **Animation Courtyard**.

10) In the back room of **Walt Disney: One Man's Dream** is an ensemble of pictures on the back wall from Disney films clustered together. Toy Story 2 is represented by a picture of Woody, Jessie, and Bullseye.

The final reference in Disney's Hollywood Studios can be found during the afternoon parade, **Block Party Bash**.

11) There are pictures of the majority of the characters from Toy Story 2 on the blocks at the front of the first float in **Block Party Bash**. The Green Army Men are found throughout the parade and act as hosts to get you in the party mood. On and around the Toy Story float is Mr. Potato Head, Woody, Buzz, Jessie, Lenny, Bo Peep, and Jessie.

Fun Fact: There are several references to "a bug's life" found throughout the film. Heimlich is on a branch that Buzz swats down, there is a display within Al's Toy Barn for the film, and during the elevator scene the elevator music is actually music from the film.

Downtown Disney

The first reference at Downtown Disney can be found in **Downtown Disney's Marketplace**.

12) While walking around **Downtown Disney's Marketplace**, listen for the song, "Woody's Roundup" from Toy Story 2. This is one of thirty-two songs played in the area so the odds of hearing it within the first few songs are pretty slim.

After finishing up at Downtown Disney's Marketplace, go to **Downtown Disney's West Side** for your next reference.

13) You can find cutouts of Buzz Lightyear and Zurg at **Buzz Lightyear's Astroblasters** within **DisneyQuest**.

Fun Fact: Toy Story 2 was originally planned to be a direct to video sequel. After seeing some of the work that was being done on the film, Disney decided it had the potential to be a successful box office movie.

Resorts

The final references to Toy Story 2 throughout Walt Disney World can be found at **All-Star Movies** and **Pop Century**.

14) After entering the **World Premiere** food court at **All-Star Movies**, take a look at the wall on the left to find a poster for Toy Story 2.

15) A picture that consists of all the toys found within the film is located between the refreshment dispensers in the **World Premiere** food court at **All-Star Movies**.

16) While coming from the lobby and heading towards the 1990's section at **Pop Century**, you can find Mr. and Mrs. Potato Head. They do not look exactly like our friends from the Toy Story films, but the looks are what inspired everyone's favorite potato couple in the film.

Fun Fact: In the original Toy Story film, no characters sang a song. In Toy Story 2, however, both Woody and Wheezy sing the popular song from the first film, "You've Got a Friend in Me."

"Fantasia 2000"

Released: January 1, 2000

The Film in Three Paragraphs

Just like its predecessor, Fantasia 2000 focuses around several stories in eight individual segments. The first segment,

"Symphony No. 5" by Ludwig van Beethoven, revolves around a series of abstract objects that closely resemble butterflies as they go from light to darkness and back to light again. The following segment of the film, "Pines of Rome" by Ottorino Respighi, follows a whale calf that gets separated from his parents. Through the magic of animation, the calf and his parents fly into space with a pod of whales.

"Rhapsody In Blue" by George Gershwin, the next segment of the film, focuses around four separate characters throughout the course of a day. The characters consist of a construction worker who wants to play music, a girl who is stuck with her nanny, an unemployed man, and a man who just wants to have fun but feels forced to be with his wife. The following segment, "Piano Concerto No. 2, Allegro, Opus 102" by Dmitri Shostakovich, tells the story of a toy soldier who gets lost, but eventually returns home to his true love. The next segment of the film, "Carnival of the Animals, finale" by Camille Saint-Saens, follows a flamingo who plays with his yo-yo much to the irritation of the other flamingos in his flock.

The next segment is a familiar one to almost everyone, "The Sorcerer's Apprentice" by Paul Dukas, which features Mickey Mouse as he attempts to use magic. "Pomp and Circumstance-Marches 1, 2, 3, and 4" by Sir Edward Elgar features Donald Duck and Daisy Duck in a retelling of the famous Noah's Ark story. The final number of the film is "Firebird Suite – 1919 Version" by Igor Stravinsky. As pointed out in the introduction by Angela Lansbury, this segment focuses on life, death, and renewal.

Magic Kingdom

Your only stop in the Magic Kingdom is on **Main Street, USA.**

1) You can find a picture of the spring girl in the "Firebird Suite" sequence of the film in the Milestones in Disney Animation, which can be found in the back room of **Exposition Hall**.

Fun Fact: Fantasia 2000 was the first animated film ever to be presented in IMAX format. The release of the film in IMAX on December 31, 1999 was one day prior to the general release.

Disney's Hollywood Studios

The only reference found throughout Disney's Hollywood Studios can be found at **Walt Disney: One Man's Dream**, which is located in the **Animation Courtyard**.

2) There is a group of pictures on the back wall of the back room in **Walt Disney: One Man's Dream**. Included in this collage is a picture of the spring girl from the "Firebird Suite" sequence of the film.

Fun Fact: "The Firebird Suite" sequence of the film was actually inspired by Roy E. Disney's trip to Mount St. Helens after its eruption. He thought it would be great to put a camera there and watch the plants grow back over 500 years. In essence, this is what happens in "The Firebird Suite" sequence of the film.

Resorts

The final group of references to Fantasia 2000 can be found at **All-Star Movies**.

3) The design of the children's pool on the left hand side of the Fantasia themed pool at **All-Star Movies** is similar to the glaciers found in the "Pines of Rome" sequence of the film.

4) In the **All-Star Movies** Fantasia themed area, look to the left of the Sorcerer Mickey pool to find a building inspired by the "Piano Concerto No. 2, Allegro, Opus 102" segment of the film. Or in simpler terms, the toy solider

scene. Here you will find a large version of our solider hero and his ballerina love. In addition to this, the evil Jack-In-The-Box takes center stage opposite of Yensid's hat.

5) If you head past the Sorcerer Mickey pool at **All-Star Movies**, you can find Donald Duck and Daisy in their Noah's Ark garments near a hammock.

Fun Fact: When the original Fantasia was in production in the late 1930's, the Disney Company actually thought about having Donald play the role of the Sorcerer's Apprentice. Thankfully, they decided against this and gave Mickey one of his most memorable roles.

"Dinosaur"

Released: May 19, 2000

The Film in Three Paragraphs

After an Iguanodon's egg is separated from its mother, it gets carried to Lemur Island where a family of lemurs finds the egg just before it hatches. When the baby Iguanodon is born, the lemurs adopt it with the hope that if it grows up with them, it will protect them when it is full grown. Years pass and the lemur family, along with the Iguanodon they now call Aladar, are living happily on Lemur Island.

During the lemur's mating ritual, a meteor shower occurs and destroys Lemur Island. Aladar and lemurs Plio, Yar, Zini, and Suri escape the island and swim safely to the main land. Shortly after they arrive, they join a herd of dinosaurs. Since most of the land is unlivable due to the meteor shower, the dinosaurs are traveling to their nesting grounds in hopes that it was not destroyed.

Aladar quickly becomes friends with the stragglers of the herd and continues to encourage them to keep moving for their survival. The leader of the herd, Kron, is upset by Aladar's helpfulness to the group in the back and forces his beautiful sister, Neera, to stay away from him.

Aladar continues to help the stragglers. They are eventually separated from the rest of the herd and become trapped inside a cave. Two Carnotaurs attack the group and force them to the back of the cave which turns out to be a tunnel that leads to the nesting grounds. Aladar, concerned about the rest of the herd, leaves the stragglers to locate and lead the rest of the group back to the nesting grounds. Kron refuses to follow Aladar and falls to his doom during a fight with a Carnotaur. In the end, the rest of the herd arrives at the nesting grounds, and Neera and Aladar welcome their new baby into the world.

Magic Kingdom

The only reference found in the Magic Kingdom is on **Main Street, USA**.

1) There is a picture of Baylene the Brachiosaurus on the Milestones in Disney Animation mural in the back room of **Exposition Hall**.

Fun Fact: The film was originally intended to have no dialogue throughout the entire film.

Disney's Animal Kingdom

The final group of references for the film can be found in **Dinoland, USA**.

2) Where can you find an obvious reference to Dinosaur? At **Dinosaur** the attraction, of course! Before entering the

queue, check out the wonderful statue of Aladar in front of the building.

3) Before riding **Dinosaur,** you will watch a quick clip from the film during the pre-show. While riding the attraction, you can find both a Carnotaur and Aladar himself. Look at the monitor screen on your right hand side after returning from the "past" to spot Aladar. You can also find clips of Aladar on the screens within the gift shop.

Fun Fact: The Dinosaur attraction existed prior to the film's release in 2000, but with a different name: Countdown to Extinction.

"The Emperor's New Groove"

Released: December 15, 2000

The Film in Three Paragraphs

When Emperor Kuzko decides to give himself a summer home for his birthday, he summons Pacha, a peasant, who lives on the hill he plans to build it on to get his opinion. After Pacha tells him what a wonderful place it is, Kuzko informs him that he plans to destroy Pacha's house to make way for his summer home. Pacha is furious. Meanwhile in the palace, evil advisor Yzma is trying to take over the kingdom with assistance from her dim witted henchman Kronk. They decide to kill Kuzko, but accidentally mix up the poison bottle with a llama potion, which turns Kuzko into a llama instead. Yzma tells Kronk to kill Kuzko, but he drops the bag that contains the Emperor down some stairs and the bag lands on Pacha's cart.

When Pacha returns home, he discovers Kuzko in llama form. Kuzko demands to be returned to the palace. Pacha says he will, but only if Kuzko agrees to build his summer home some-where else. Kuzko stubbornly leaves and instantly gets into trouble. Kind-hearted Pacha comes to his rescue and saves him. The two continue on their journey to the palace. They stop at a diner for lunch, see Yzma and Kronk, and realize that they are trying to kill Kuzko.

Pacha and Kuzko rush back to the palace with Kronk and Yzma right on their heels. When Pacha and Kuzko finally arrive, they find the other two in Yzma's secret lair waiting for them. There is a mad dash for the potion that will turn Kuzko back into a human. In the end, Kuzko and Pacha find the right potion and Kuzko returns to his normal body. A thankful Kuzko decides to build his summer home next to Pacha's house and works on being a better person and emperor.

Disney's Hollywood Studios

The only two references found throughout all of Walt Disney World can be found in the **Animation Courtyard**.

1) The **Magic of Disney Animation** building is home to the interactive game **Digital Ink and Paint**, which is hosted by Kronk.

2) If you head to the back room of **Walt Disney: One Man's Dream**, you can find a group of pictures on the back wall. The Emperor's New Groove is represented here by one of the movie posters for the film.

Fun Fact: John Fiedler provided the voice for both Rudy, the old man who Kuzko throws out the window, and the voice for Piglet in the Winnie the Pooh films. The Emperor's New Groove was one of the last films John Fiedler ever worked on.

"Atlantis: The Lost Empire"

Released: June 8, 2001

The Film in Three Paragraphs

After linguist Milo Thatch's proposal to have an expedition to find the lost city of Atlantis is rejected, he receives an offer from his grandfather's old friend, Mr. Whitmore. Mr. Whitmore gives Milo The Shepard's Journal, a tool to help find Atlantis, and agrees to finance the expedition, and soon Milo is underway on the exploration to rediscover Atlantis. Shortly after they begin their journey, the expedition team, under the leadership of Commander Lyle Rourke, encounter an underwater beast, which kills the majority of the crew.

Milo leads the remaining crew members to the legendary city. They soon come face to face with real people, which is shocking since they believed the entire civilization was dead. The first Atlantean they meet is Princess Kida. Her father, the king, wants them to leave, but Kida wants answers. She is trying to figure out why their civilization is slowly dying and, since no one is able to read the language, she enlists the help of Milo.

After Milo realizes the crystals the citizens use are the lifeline for the city, Commander Rourke takes over and threatens the lives of the Atlantean people so he can turn a profit with the find. They discover the main crystal, which claims Kida's body and turns her into the city's lifeline. Rourke loads Kida into the truck and drives away. Milo leads a rescue party to fight Rourke and to return Kida to her people. After a furious battle, Rourke meets his doom and Milo restores life to Atlantis by returning Kida to the city. Kida reclaims her human form and Milo decides to remain in Atlantis and live with her.

Magic Kingdom

The first reference to Atlantis can be discovered on **Main Street, USA.**

1) There is a picture of Dr. Sweet, who is in fact not a cookie, on the Milestones in Disney Animation collage in the back room of **Exposition Hall.**

Fun Fact: The film was originally going to have a television series spin off, but since the film was not as popular as expected, the idea was cancelled. Some of the episode ideas were put into the film's sequel, "Atlantis: Milo's Return."

Disney's Hollywood Studios

The next two references to Atlantis can both be found in the **Animation Courtyard** area.

2) While in the main show at the **Magic of Disney Animation,** look around the room. On the shelf directly behind the drawing of Mushu are a variety of toys from the film Atlantis: The Lost Empire. It appears the collection is complete and all of the main characters are accounted for.

3) The back wall of the back room in **Walt Disney: One Man's Dream** contains an ensemble of pictures from Disney films grouped together in one section including Atlantis: The Lost Empire. The movie is represented by the film's poster.

Fun Fact: Dr. Marc Okrand, an American linguist who is most famous for creating the Klingon language, was hired to help create the Atlantean language for the film.

Resorts

The final reference can be found at the **World Premiere** food court in **All-Star Movies**.

4) While facing the "Lyric" section of the **World Premiere** food court in **All-Star Movies**, take a look to your right to find a few pictures from the film within a film reel.

"Monsters, Inc."

Released: November 2, 2001

The Film in Three Paragraphs

Monsters, Inc. is a company in the monster world that generates power from the screams of children in the human world. One day, top scarer James P. Sullivan, or Sulley for short, finds a door to the human world unattended and accidentally lets a child from the human world into the monster world. The monsters believe that children from the human world are toxic and extremely deadly creatures so when the citizens of Monstropolis catch sight of the child, a major panic occurs throughout the city.

With help from his best friend Mike Wazowski, Sulley sets out to return the child, that he has named Boo, back to the human world. When Randall, a villainous scarer who works for Monsters, Inc., approaches Mike about giving him Boo, the two friends realize Randall is trying to kidnap Boo so he can become the top scarer. Mike and Sulley approach the company's owner, Mr. Waternoose, and inform him of the fiendish plot. Unfortunately for them, Mr. Waternoose is also in on the plot and banishes the two to the Himalayas.

With Mike upset about Sulley's devotion to Boo, he turns on his friend and lets Sulley leave without him. Sulley returns to the monster world and locates Boo. Mr. Waternoose follows Sulley into a room that, unknown to Waternoose, is being recorded by officials with Mike's assistance. Waternoose admits that he would kidnap children before he would let his company fail. Waternoose is taken away, Boo is returned home, and everyone at Monsters, Inc. is put out of work. Sulley realizes they do not need to scare children to attain energy, but instead they can make children laugh to receive even more energy since laughter is ten times more powerful than screams. The company is changed into a comedy club brought to human children around the world and energy becomes plentiful in the monster world.

Magic Kingdom

Your first stop is on **Main Street, USA** and don't worry, it's not a scary one.

1) There is a picture of Mike and Sulley together in the Milestones in Disney Animation display in the back room of **Exposition Hall**.

The biggest, and some would say the best, reference to the film is found in **Tomorrowland**.

2) Mike Wazowski developed a plan to help bring more energy to the monster world by creating a place called **Monsters, Inc. Laugh Floor**. The premise behind the Laugh Floor is that instead of having the monsters enter our world, we enter theirs. The pre-show recaps the movie with scenes from the film that feature characters such as Sulley and Boo. Roz and Mike are also in the video explaining the purpose of the Laugh Floor.

3) There are several fun references to the film in the waiting area for **Monsters, Inc. Laugh Floor**. One of the greatest treasures is the bulletin board that has notes from the characters in the film (and their loved ones) along with reviews of the show including one by Celia, who still claims Mike as her googli-bear.

4) During the **Monsters, Inc. Laugh Floor** show, you are guaranteed to see Roz and Mike. Other than that, anything is up in the air. The show is never the same twice, and each show you have the chance to meet some new monsters. Since the show is always different, try to visit it a few times during your trip for new jokes, new monsters, and more fun.

5) While riding the **Tomorrowland Transit Authority** keep your ears open as you pass the Laugh Floor to hear Roz!

Fun Fact: Monsters, Inc. Laugh Floor did not have a home in Tomorrowland until April 2, 2007. The previous attraction in this location was The Timekeeper, which ran from 1994 until 2006.

Disney's Hollywood Studios

You can find your first reference in Disney's Hollywood Studios near the **Streets of America**.

6) **Character Meet and Greet Alert!** While facing the Backlot Tour at the end of the **Streets of America**, you will find a door on your right hand side. This is the entrance for the character meet and greet for Sulley and Mike. The queue has some posters on the wall in the glass case. Included in the case are some of the magazine articles that Roz was reading in the film and a few other good finds.

Fun Fact: In Disney's California Adventure, there is an attraction based off the film called Monsters, Inc. Mike & Sulley to the Rescue!

Your next stop in Disney's Hollywood Studios is at **Walt Disney: One Man's Dream** in the **Animation Courtyard**.

7) A Monsters, Inc. poster is included in a group of pictures on the back wall of the back room in **Walt Disney: One Man's Dream**.

Fun Fact: John Ratzenberger, who provides a voice in each Pixar film, provided the voice of The Abominable Snowman.

The final reference throughout Walt Disney World is during **Block Party Bash**.

8) During Disney's Hollywood Studios daily parade, **Block Party Bash**, you can find the majority of the characters from the film partying in the street including Sulley, Mike, Boo, the two teenage guys, and even George!

Fun Fact: Billy Crystal was originally offered the role of Buzz Lightyear in Toy Story, but turned it down. He regretted the decision after he saw the film and asked Pixar to give him a role in a future film. Pixar agreed and he was cast for the role of Mike Wazowski.

"Lilo and Stitch"

Released: June 21, 2002

The Film in Three Paragraphs

After mad scientist Jumba invents Experiment 626, a super weapon that is nearly indestructible, he is put in jail, while 626, a little blue alien, is sent to exile on a meteor. On the way to his exile, 626 escapes in a small ship and enters hyper drive which sends him on a direct course to Earth. Meanwhile on Earth, a little girl named

Lilo is down on her luck. Her sister Nani and she are alone after the death of their parents and Lilo is having trouble making friends. In addition, Lilo is going to be taken away from Nani if Nani does not fulfill her new motherly responsibilities.

626, in the mean time, crash lands in Hawaii and is run over. Being mistaken for a dog, he is taken to the pound. Nani decides that letting Lilo adopt a pet will provide the friend she is seeking so the two visit the dog pound. Lilo finds 626, adopts him, and names him Stitch. Unfortunately for Lilo, Stitch wrecks everything he touches and just wants to cause trouble. Nani tries to get rid of Stitch, but Lilo insists that he is family even if he has only been a member for a short time.

Jobless Nani is told by a social worker, Cobra Bubbles, that he is going to take Lilo away from her the following day due to an unsafe living environment. The next day while Nani is interviewing for a job, aliens try to recapture Stitch and attack Lilo and Stitch at the house. The two are captured, but Stitch manages to escape. In the end, Stitch rescues Lilo and, since she paid for him, the aliens decide that Stitch is the sole property of Lilo. In addition, they put Lilo and Nani's family under galactic protection so they can never be separated.

Magic Kingdom

Amazingly enough, the first reference to Lilo and Stitch is found in **Frontierland**.

1) Inside the **Frontier Trading Post** are wanted posters for two Disney characters. Stitch is sticking his head into the upper right hand corner of the picture offering a $1,000 reward for the capture of Brer Fox.

For several references to the film, head over to **Tomorrowland**.

2) The first attraction on your left hand side after entering Tomorrowland from Main Street, USA is **Stitch's Great Escape**. You will know you are in the right place when you see Stitch on the sign outside. Agent Pleakley and Captain Gantu can both be found during the pre-show. During the attraction, you can find the Grand Councilwoman and Stitch in addition to Pleakley and Gantu. Please note that children who love the film may become frightened by this very dark attraction.

Fun Fact: Stitch's Great Escape took the place of the popular attraction The ExtraTERRORestrial Alien Encounter, which ran from June 20, 1995 through October 12, 2003.

3) You can find Stitch in the mural that is on the ceiling of **Mickey's Star Traders**.

4) While inside **Merchant of Venus**, you can find Stitch popping out of the ceiling.

5) There is a robotic Paperboy selling newspapers between the entrances of the **Tomorrowland Transit Authority** and the **Astro Orbitor**. If you look at the lead story of the newspaper he is carrying, you will see that it focuses around Stitch's escape!

6) While riding the Tomorrowland Transit Authority, keep your ears open as you pass Stitch's Great Escape to hear Stitch!

7) **Character Meet and Greet Alert!** You can have your picture taken with Stitch at certain times throughout the day near the right hand side of the **Carousel of Progress**.

Fun Fact: While Nani is looking for a job during the film, you can find Cinderella Castle on a postcard in the background. This comes full circle during Stitch's Great Escape when Stitch is creating havoc around the Magic Kingdom, most notably at Cinderella Castle.

Epcot

The only reference to Lilo and Stitch can be found in **Future World**.

8) **Character Meet and Greet Alert!** Stitch is occasionally available for photo opportunities outside of **Mission: SPACE**.

Fun Fact: You can find a poster for Mulan above Nani's bed during the film.

Disney's Hollywood Studios

The first group of references in Disney's Hollywood Studios can be found in the **Animation Courtyard**.

9) During the **Magic of Disney Animation** show with Mushu, there are a variety of small items from different Disney films on the desk behind your host. On the very top of this desk is what appears to be a bobble head of Lilo on the left hand side.

10) Just after exiting the **Magic of Disney Animation** show with Mushu, you can find a glass display case of the newest animated films. If you look to your left, you can find background drawings that were used for Lilo and Stitch.

11) After taking a look at the background drawings for the film in the **Magic of Disney Animation,** you will pass two offices before arriving to the interactive game area. In the first office are a variety of small knick knacks from various Disney films including an Elvis impersonating Stitch toy with guitar in hand on the desk.

12) The same office in the **Magic of Disney Animation** contains another Stitch decked out in beach clothes with a surfboard in hand high on the desk.

13) Before entering the **Animation Academy** in the **Magic of Disney Animation**, take a look at the pencil drawings on the wall. Two of the characters included are Lilo and Stitch.

14) Take a look at the left hand wall after entering the **Animation Academy** located inside the **Magic of Disney Animation** building to find sketches demonstrating how to draw Stitch.

The final reference in Disney's Hollywood Studios can be found during **Fantasmic!**

15) There are a wide variety of characters on the steamboat with Mickey at the end of **Fantasmic!** including Lilo and Stitch who are present the majority of the time.

Fun Fact: Lilo and Stitch is the second of only three Disney Animated Features to have all production of the film done at the Animation Studio in Florida. The other two are Mulan and Brother Bear.

Disney's Animal Kingdom

The only reference to the film in Disney's Animal Kingdom can be found on **Discovery Island**.

16) **Character Meet and Greet Alert!** You can meet Lilo and Stitch at certain times throughout the day near the **Disney Vacation Club** area that is across from **Pizzafari**.

Fun Fact: During the early developmental stages of the story, the film team considered having the film take place in "isolated" Kansas.

Downtown Disney

The first two references in **Downtown Disney's Marketplace** can be found at **World of Disney**.

17) There is a giant Stitch above the **World of Disney** entrance that is closest to the Ghiradelhi Chocolate Shop. Watch out! He does spit!

18) Take a look inside some of the windows to the right of the spitting Stitch while still outside of **World of Disney** to find a giant comic book featuring Lilo, Stitch, Jumba, Pleakley, David, and even Mertle Edmonds!

19) While walking around **Downtown Disney's Marketplace**, you may hear the song "Hawaiian Roller Coaster Ride" from the film being played.

Fun Fact: Due to the popularity of the film, three direct to video sequels were made ("Stitch! The Movie," "Lilo and Stitch 2: Stitch has a Glitch," and "Leroy and Stitch"). In addition to the sequels, a television series, "Lilo and Stitch: The Series," was created.

Water Parks

The only water park to host a reference to Lilo and Stitch is **Typhoon Lagoon**.

20) **Character Meet and Greet Alert!** While in **Typhoon Lagoon**, keep an eye out for Lilo and Stitch who may be available for meet and greets. Please note they are not always present so make sure you ask a cast member if they will be available to meet during your stay.

Fun Fact: Although Pleakley only has one eye, he does have two tongues and three legs.

Resorts

The final two references to the film can be found at the **Polynesian** resort.

21) You can find a statue of Lilo and Stitch in the **Kona Café**, which is located in the **Polynesian Resort**.

22) There is a Lilo and Stitch surfboard located near the Disney Vacation Club booth in the front lobby of the **Polynesian**.

23) **Character Meet and Greet Alert!** The final reference for the film can be found at the **'Ohana's Best Friends Breakfast with Lilo and Stitch** inside the **Polynesian** resort where you can join Lilo and Stitch for breakfast.

Fun Fact: 'Ohana means family in Hawaiian, but not just in the traditional sense. It also refers to close friends and neighbors.

"Treasure Planet"

Released: November 27, 2002

The Film in Three Paragraphs

The film begins with a young Jim Hawkins who is enthralled with a book about Treasure Planet. He believes it is real, but his mom tries to convince him it is more like a legend. Twelve years pass and Jim is consistently getting in trouble with the police. When a man named Billy Bones crashes on his mother's dock, Jim receives a treasure map and a warning from Billy, "Beware the cyborg." The cyborg and his crew quickly arrive and burn down Jim's mother's Inn.

After figuring out how to read the map, Jim and his family friend, Dr. Delbert Doppler, set out to retrieve the treasure. The two soon arrive at the ship the R.S.L. Legacy, and Jim is assigned to be the cook's cabin boy. The cook, John Silver, is a cyborg and assigns Jim an extensive amount of work. While the two work together, they begin to bond. Jim, however, overhears Silver and the rest of the crew talking about mutiny. Jim informs the Captain what he overheard, and they quickly escape the ship of mutinous sailors with Dr. Doppler.

After reaching Treasure Planet, they realize they had left the map on the ship. The pirates soon arrive still believing that Jim and the others possess the map. Jim sneaks back onboard the ship, retrieves the map, but when he returns, he finds his friends have been captured. Jim reluctantly leads Silver and his crew to the treasure. In the process, they set off an alarm that will destroy the entire planet. With some quick thinking, Jim rescues his friends and the remaining pirates and returns them safely home. Silver decides to attempt an escape before being sent to jail. Jim, seeing some change in Silver, lets him go. In return for his freedom, Silver gives Jim some coins from the treasure, which allows Jim and his mother to restore their Inn back to its former glory.

Downtown Disney

The only reference to Treasure Planet is debatable and can be found in **World of Disney.**

1) **That's Debatable!** If you enter **World of Disney** through the doors below Stitch, you will find yourself in the "Adventure Room." There is artwork above the right hand shelving units just before the doorway to the dishes and coffee room. If you look closely at the design of the space artwork, you will see an "X" as in "X marks the spot." However, there is nothing specific to Treasure Planet. Some people I have discussed this with believe this is a

reference to the film, while others believe it is just a coincidence. One thing to keep in mind while trying to decide if this is a reference to the film is the theme of the room. Since this is located in the "pirate room" of the store, I believe this is in fact a reference to "Treasure Planet."

Fun Fact: John Silver's cyborg parts are computer animated, but the rest of his body was created by traditional hand drawn animation.

"Finding Nemo"

Released: May 30, 2003

The Film in Three Paragraphs

A clownfish named Nemo disobeys his father and is captured by a diver. His father, Marlin, begins to swim frantically after the boat that carries the diver and his son, but he is unable to keep up. While looking for help, he meets a fish with short-term memory loss named Dory who eagerly wants to help, but continues to forget what she was doing. The two of them soon discover a mask, which belonged to the diver that took Nemo away. Dory reads the mask and learns it says, "P. Sherman, 42 Wallaby Way, Sydney."

Meanwhile, Nemo has been taken to the diver's office where he learns he will be the birthday present for the diver's niece who has a reputation for killing fish. With the help of the fellow fish in the tank, they develop a plan to escape and reach the ocean. Unfortunately, their plan fails and Nemo is devastated that he is unable to return to the ocean and his father. Back in the ocean, Marlin and Dory are overcoming sharks, sea monsters, jelly fish forests, and a whale. Marlin shares his journey with a group of sea turtles and the story is quickly retold across the ocean and reaches

Sydney harbor. In the harbor, a pelican named Nigel hears the story and shares it with the fish tank gang that Nemo is residing with.

Marlin and Dory finally arrive in Sydney. At the same time, Nemo is being removed from the fish tank and given to Darla, the diver's niece. Nemo fakes his death so he will be flushed down the toilet, which will lead him back to the ocean. Nigel carries Marlin and Dory to the office just in time to also be fooled by Nemo's act of playing dead. Devastated, they turn away and leave. Nemo, alive and well, exits the drain into the ocean and meets Dory, who has just been separated from Marlin. The two decide to look for Marlin together until Dory suddenly makes the connection that this is Nemo, Marlin's son. Marlin and Nemo are finally reunited and return to their home on the reef with their new friend Dory.

Epcot

There are no references found in the Magic Kingdom so head over to **Future World** in Epcot for your first group of references.

1) Outside of **The Seas with Nemo and Friends** are Nemo, Marlin, Dory, the fish tank gang, and a few of Nemo's school friends on display. Also before entering the building, you can find the talkative seagulls.

2) The queue for **The Seas with Nemo and Friends** is one of the most detailed found throughout Walt Disney World. The main references to look for while in line are the school of fish that display new pictures for you on one of the walls and the bottom of the "butt."

3) During **The Seas with Nemo and Friends Attraction**, you can find all of the major underwater characters throughout the film including Nemo, Marlin, Dory, Crush, and many more!

4) After exiting **The Seas with Nemo and Friends Attraction**, take a look around the building. You can find characters such as Bruce, Anchor, and Chum throughout the building highlighting educational facts about different types of sharks and fish.

5) While still in **The Seas with Nemo and Friends**, head over to **Turtle Talk with Crush**. There are fun facts about Nemo, his fish tank friends, and some of his school mates in the lobby area.

6) During **Turtle Talk with Crush**, inside **The Seas with Nemo and Friends**, you will meet Crush himself. Thanks to some new technology, the audience is able to actually talk and interact with Crush. Since each performance of the show is different, you never know who you will see. Several characters from the film appear at times including Dory, Squirt, and even the whale!

Fun Fact: If you love Dory, you should visit the Universe of Energy. Ellen DeGeneres, who provided the voice of Dory, is the hostess for this Future World attraction.

Disney's Hollywood Studios

The only reference found in Disney's Hollywood Studios is in the **Animation Courtyard**.

7) While in the **Magic of Disney Animation** show with Mushu, take a look around the room to find a variety of small items from different Disney films. In a room full of references, it is hard to find a certain clown fish. However, behind the drawing of Mushu is a PEZ dispenser of Nemo!

Fun Fact: John Ratzenberger, who provides a voice in each Pixar film, provided the voice of the spokesman for the school of fish.

Disney's Animal Kingdom

There is only one reference in Disney's Animal Kingdom, but it is my personal favorite reference for Finding Nemo. It can be found just outside of **Dinoland, USA**.

8) **Finding Nemo: The Musical** is performing in the Theater in the Wild, which is located just outside of Dinoland, USA. This amazing show features all of your favorite characters including Nemo, Marlin, Dory, Crush, Squirt, and even Nigel. This show is a must "sea" for all fans of Nemo or live theatre.

Fun Fact: Finding Nemo: The Musical was written by Tony Award winning composer Robert Lopez.

Downtown Disney

The final reference can be heard throughout **Downtown Disney's Marketplace**.

9) While walking around **Downtown Disney's Marketplace**, listen for the song "Beyond the Sea" from the closing credits of Finding Nemo. This is one of thirty-two songs played in the area, so the odds of hearing it within the first few songs are pretty slim.

Fun Fact: To help make the underwater scenes of the film look more believable, John Lasseter, the head of Pixar, had everyone working on the film become scuba certified.

"Brother Bear"

Released: October 24, 2003

The Film in Three Paragraphs

After three brothers return from fishing, the youngest brother, Kenai, carelessly leaves the fish on the ground. This allows a bear and her cub to retrieve the fish. When the brothers return to find the fish missing, Kenai hunts down the bear. The bear reacts by attacking Kenai. Kenai's brothers come to his aid, but his brother Sitka dies in the brawl. Kenai blames the bear for his brother's death and heads off to kill the bear once and for all. Kenai defeats the bear, and Sitka, now in the form of a spirit, turns Kenai into a bear to learn a lesson.

Denahi, Kenai's remaining brother, believes the bear, who is actually Kenai, has killed Kenai as well and seeks vengeance on the bear. Kenai escapes and encounters the tribal shaman who informs him that in order to return to human form, he must reach the spot where the lights touch the earth. Kenai meets a bear named Koda who is headed to a salmon run, which just happens to be next to the location where the lights touch the earth. Therefore, the two set out on the journey together. At first, Koda comes off as annoying to Kenai. However, they begin to bond when Kenai starts to understand that Koda sees man as a monster and not the other way around.

Once the two reach the salmon run, Koda tells the other bears about a battle his mother had with a hunter. While telling the story, Kenai realizes he was the hunter that killed Koda's mother and confesses to the young cub. A hurt Koda runs away. While trying to find Koda, Kenai is attacked by Denahi. Just before Denahi stabs Kenai, Sitka uses his magical powers to turn Kenai back into a human. The three brothers are happy to be reunited, but Kenai realizes that Koda needs him and asks to be turned back into a bear. In the end, Kenai proves to his tribe that he has become a man by turning into a bear.

Epcot

The only reference found in Epcot is in **World Showcase**.

1) **Character Meet and Greet Alert!** On rare occasion, you can meet Kenai and Koda in the **Canada** pavilion. It is best to ask a cast member if these two will be available during your visit since their appearances are very rare.

Fun Fact: To help capture the look of the North American wilderness, the animators took a research trip to Denali National Park and Yosemite National Park.

Disney's Hollywood Studios

All three references in Disney's Hollywood Studios can be found in the **Magic of Disney Animation** building in the **Animation Courtyard**.

2) Kenai's Bear of Love totem is on the left hand side of the room where the **Magic of Disney Animation** show takes place.

3) You can find background sketches from Brother Bear on the walls of the room where the **Magic of Disney Animation** show occurs.

4) Near the **Animation Academy** line in the **Magic of Disney Animation** building is a large pencil sketch of Kenai and Koda drawn upon the wall.

Fun Fact: When Kenai wakes up as a bear, the screen actually widens to represent the fact that he is seeing the world from a new perspective.

Disney's Animal Kingdom

The final reference found in Walt Disney World is in **Camp Minnie-Mickey**.

5) **Character Meet and Greet Alert!** At certain times throughout the year, you can meet Kenai and Koda on the **Character Greeting Trails** in Camp Minnie-Mickey. Please note these are not the only characters found on the trails, and they may not be available to meet during your visit. Ask a cast member on specific times to meet these characters.

"The Incredibles"

Released: November 5, 2004

The Film in Three Paragraphs

Fifteen years after Supers are forced to live their lives as ordinary citizens, Bob Parr, formerly known as Mr. Incredible, wants to relive the glory days of being a super hero. When asked to defeat a robot that has taken over an island, Bob jumps at the opportunity and defeats the robot with little difficulty. After being able to use his true talents again, Bob feels more alive and begins to pay more attention to his family, which he has been neglecting.

Bob is asked to return to the island a second time. However, his wife Helen, formerly Elastigirl, becomes suspicious of his whereabouts. She finds Bob's old Super uniform, notices it has recently been mended, and realizes that he has been fighting crime. Helen calls Edna Mode, designer of super hero uniforms, and learns Edna has made new super hero uniforms for Helen and all three of her children. When Helen inquires about Bob's location,

Edna pushes a button that activates Bob's location beacon and highlights where Bob is currently at in the world. The button also gives away Mr. Incredible's location on the island to his enemy, resulting in his capture by a sidekick he once rejected named Syndrome.

Helen flies to the island to rescue Bob, but soon realizes that two of her children, Dash and Violet, have snuck on board as well. Syndrome learns they are coming and shoots the plane out of the sky, but not before the three are able to escape. The family arrives on the island, saves Bob, but are captured together before they can escape the island. Syndrome informs them he plans to attack the city with the robot he created and then save the city by defeating it. He assumes he will then be praised for his rescue and will be able to sell his gadgets to everyone so anyone can be a Super. The family foils his plans by escaping, returning to the city, and defeating the robot together. In the end, the world is happy to have the Supers back, but, more importantly, the family begins to treat one another with more respect.

Disney's Hollywood Studios

The first reference found throughout Walt Disney World is in the **Animation Courtyard**.

1) **Character Meet and Greet Alert!** You can meet Frozone and Mr. and Mrs. Incredible inside the **Magic of Disney Animation** building near the interactive game area.

Fun Fact: Brad Bird, who wrote and directed the film, provided the voice of Edna Mode.

The final reference in Disney's Hollywood Studios can be found during the daily parade, **Block Party Bash**.

2) If you stay for the finale of **Block Party Bash**, you can find all of the Incredibles on separate floats. Please take

note the only time to find these characters during the entire celebration is at the very end.

Fun Fact: John Ratzenberger, who has provided a voice in every Pixar film, provided the voice of the Underminer, the super villain who pops up at the end of the film.

Downtown Disney

The first reference in **Downtown Disney's Marketplace** can be found on the outside of **World of Disney**

3) If you look into the outside windows between the Stitch entrance and the Mickey and Minnie entrance of **World of Disney**, you can find some giant comic book pages. One of these comic books follows the adventures of our favorite super hero family.

4) While walking around **Downtown Disney's Marketplace**, listen for the main theme song from the film. This is one of thirty-two songs that is played in the area.

Fun Fact: A new cartoon titled "Jack-Jack Attack" was added to the DVD to show audiences what was going on with Jack-Jack and babysitter Kari while the rest of the family was on the island.

"Chicken Little"

Released: November 4, 2005

The Film in Three Paragraphs

A year after Chicken Little scares the town by proclaiming the sky is falling, he and his father are still being humiliated on a daily basis by constant reminders of the incident. Chicken Little is looked down upon by almost everyone in his school and his father is disappointed in him. Knowing his dad's success in baseball, Chicken Little decides to join the baseball team to make his father proud. No one on the team has confidence in him, and the coach never gives him a chance to play.

During the championship game, most of the team becomes injured and the outcome of the game rests in Chicken Little's hands. After two strikes, the town is horrified they will lose the big game. Instead, Chicken Little comes through with an infield home run and becomes the town hero. That night as he celebrates in his room, the sky falls once again on Chicken Little and he quickly calls upon his friends for help.

When his friend, Fish Out of Water, pushes a button, the piece of the sky and Fish travel to the baseball field to reveal a spaceship. The remaining friends board the spaceship and rescue Fish. As they escape, the alien's baby, Kirby, follows them off the ship. The aliens believe Chicken Little and his friends have kidnapped Kirby so they attack the planet Earth until Chicken Little returns Kirby to his parents. In the end, the aliens restore Earth back to its normal state and the town finally realizes that Chicken Little was not crazy, but is, in fact, a hero.

Magic Kingdom

The only reference in Walt Disney World can be found at **Mickey's Toontown Fair**.

1) There are magazine covers that have been enlarged to poster size in the hallway of **Minnie's Country House**. If you look at issue 41-x, you will notice that Chicken Little has written an article for that particular issue. Read the front cover to find out what Chicken Little has to say.

Fun Fact: The original plan was for Chicken Little to be a girl in the film.

"Cars"

Released: June 9, 2006

The Film in Three Paragraphs

The film begins with the race for the Piston Cup. The three main contenders racing for the title are veteran driver, The King, the runner-up, Chick Hicks, and rookie sensation, Lightning McQueen. The end of the race is a photo finish and a three-way tie is confirmed between the three contenders. It is decided the three will race a week later on the other side of the country. Lightning McQueen wants to win over a sponsor so he leaves immediately and forces his truck to drive straight through the night. During the night, however, his truck, Mack, falls asleep and Lightning falls out and becomes lost.

Lightning drives off the interstate in hopes of finding Mack, but instead is chased by a police car for speeding. During the pursuit, Lightning tears up and destroys the primary road through a small town called Radiator Springs. As a penalty, Lightning is sentenced to repave the road. Lightning reluctantly obeys orders at first, but slowly begins to make friendships with everyone in town, except an old racing car named Doc Hudson. After the road is repaired, Lightning fixes up the town to show his gratitude for everyone's hospitality.

Doc, believing Lightning to be just a race car punk, calls the media and notifies them on Lightning's whereabouts. The media and Mack soon arrive in Radiator Springs, pick up Lightning, and quickly leave for the final Piston Cup race. While racing,

Lightning keeps thinking about his new friends as he sits in third place. In the middle of the race, Doc comes over his radio and lets Lightning know he will be his new crew chief. Lightning, excited to have his friends with him, flies into the lead. Just before he finishes, The King crashes. Lightning, realizing that winning is not everything, turns around (allowing Chick Hicks to win) and helps The King cross the finish line. In the end, Lightning returns to Radiator Springs and brings life back to the previously forgotten town.

Disney's Hollywood Studios

The only reference in Disney's Hollywood Studios can be found near the San Francisco portion of **Streets of America**.

1) **Character Meet and Greet Alert!** Take a left at the end of the San Francisco street in the **Streets of America** to find Luigi's Casa Della Tires where you can meet Lightning McQueen and Mater.

Fun Fact: If you take a look at the blimp and tires used throughout the film, you will notice they are actually provided by the company "Lightyear," a nod to Buzz Lightyear.

Downtown Disney

The only other reference in Walt Disney World can be found while walking around **Downtown Disney's Marketplace**.

2) While walking around **Downtown Disney's Marketplace**, listen for the song "Life is a Highway" from the film. This is one of thirty-two songs that is played in this area so the odds of hearing the song within the first few are pretty slim.

Fun Fact: At the end of the film, Pixar pokes fun at the fact that they use John Ratzenberger in each of their films. During the end credits, you can find Mack, voiced by Ratzenberger, watching a variety of movies. The movies are Toy Car Story (where he voices the Piggy Truck), Monster Trucks, Inc. (where he voices the Abominable Snowplow), and A Bug's Life (where he voices P.T. Flea in car form). Mack points out that they are "just usin' the same actor over and over." The studio also brought back the voice actors of the other characters in the scenes to read their lines from the original films once more, but with a "car" twist to the dialogue.

"Meet the Robinsons"

Released: March 30, 2007

The Film in Three Paragraphs

After young Lewis is convinced he can find his birth mother, he invents a memory scanner so he can remember what she looks like and use the information to find her. While preparing to demonstrate his invention at the school science fair, a boy named Wilbur warns him to look out for a man wearing a bowler hat. The bowler hat, named Doris, ruins Lewis' project so Lewis decides to give up on his dream. Wilbur informs Lewis he is from the future and begs him to fix the invention. Lewis, not believing Wilbur is from the future, will not agree to it. Trying to convince Lewis, Wilbur shows him the time machine he came in and takes him to the future.

Once in the future, Lewis meets Wilbur's family and quickly falls in love with them realizing they are exactly the type of family he has always been searching for. Meanwhile in the past, Bowler Hat Guy attempts to sell Lewis' invention as his own, but he does not know how to turn it on. Bowler Hat Guy returns to the future in hopes of capturing Lewis to fix the invention, but the Robinsons pull together to save Lewis. Just after the successful rescue, they realize Lewis is actually the father of the family from the past and try to convince him to return home. Lewis, hurt he can not stay, runs away and encounters Bowler Hat Guy who convinces Lewis to return to the past with him.

Bowler Hat Guy then reveals that Lewis is in fact Wilbur's father, and Lewis realizes Bowler Hat Guy is actually his childhood roommate, Goob. Goob has been seeking revenge because Lewis kept him up all night years earlier causing Goob to lose a baseball game the following day. In Goob's quest for payback, he met Doris, a bowler hat that had been rejected by future Lewis as a bad invention. Lewis realizes the future will be terrible with Doris in control, so he announces to her that he will never invent her which causes her to disintegrate. Lewis fixes the memory scanner, returns to the science fair, and realizes one of the judges is Lucille, his future self's mother. Lewis, finally realizing where he belongs, is adopted by Lucille and her husband and grows up to be a great inventor.

Disney's Hollywood Studios

The only reference to the film can be found in the **Animation Courtyard**.

1) There are a variety of small items from different Disney films in the room that hosts the main show at the **Magic of Disney Animation**. If you look on a shelf behind the drawing of Mushu, you can find a PEZ dispenser of Bowler Hat Guy.

Fun Fact: When Lewis and Wilbur first arrive in the future, they travel past a place called Todayland. Todayland features Space Mountain and the Astro Orbitor, much like the Magic Kingdom's Tomorrowland.

"Ratatouille"

Released: June 29, 2007

The Film in Three Paragraphs

Remy, a rat with a highly developed sense of smell and taste, is separated from his family and ends up in Paris, France. Remy quickly realizes he is near the famous deceased chef Gusteau's restaurant. While observing the work going on in the kitchen, he sees the new garbage boy, Linguini, messing with the soup and making it much worse than it should be. Remy heads down to the kitchen and fixes the mistake, but is caught by Linguini in the process. Before Linguini gets rid of Remy, the soup is delivered to a table in the restaurant and the customers end up loving it.

Believing that Linguini made the soup, head chef Skinner forces him to remake the soup the same way the following day, doubting he will be able to duplicate it. Knowing that Remy was the creator of the soup, Linguini asks Remy for help. After the success of the soup, Remy realizes he can never be a great chef since he is a rat, while Linguini can not be a great chef since he can not cook. Therefore, the two decide to work together. Meanwhile, Skinner learns that Linguini is actually the son of Gusteau and will receive sole possession of the restaurant at the end of the month, but only if Linguini realizes and requests it.

Remy stumbles across the fact that Linguini is the rightful heir to the restaurant and retrieves the papers for Linguini. He is also reunited with his brother who informs him that his family has been in Paris all along. Meanwhile, the newly unemployed Skinner calls the health inspector to report a rat problem in order to get revenge. Linguini, however, has bigger problems on his plate. Anton Ego, a famous food critic, is scheduled to review the restaurant. When Linguini decides to inform his staff about Remy being the true cook, they all leave except Linguini's girlfriend Colette.

With the help of Remy's family, they serve up ratatouille, which Ego loves. However, the health inspector arrives and closes down the restaurant. In the end, Linguini creates a new restaurant and makes Remy the head chef. The name of the restaurant is none other than Ratatouille.

Epcot

The only reference to the film can be found in **World Showcase**.

1) **Character Meet and Greet Alert!** While in the **France** pavilion, enjoy a meal at the restaurant **Les Chefs de France**. It is here where you can meet Remy, the smallest character for Disney's new Living Character initiative. Please note that you need to book reservations for Les Chefs De France as far in advance as possible as it is difficult to attain a table during certain times of the year.

Fun Fact: John Ratzenberger, who provides the voice of a character in each Pixar film, played the part of Mustafa, the head waiter in the restaurant.

"WALL-E"

Released: June 27, 2008

The Film in Three Paragraphs

About 700 years after humans have left Earth due to an overpopulation of garbage, a robot named WALL-E (Waste Allocation Load Lifter Earth-Class) is the last remaining working robot on Earth. Each day is the same for WALL-E: he gathers garbage, compacts it, stacks it, finds and collects interesting items, and then returns home to recharge his battery. One day a spaceship arrives on Earth and drops off a robot named EVE (Extraterrestrial Vegetation Evaluator), whom WALL-E instantly becomes fascinated with. The two begin to spend all of their time together and WALL-E decides to give a plant he found to EVE as a gift. As soon as EVE sees it, she puts it in her storage unit and falls into a hyper sleep.

A spaceship arrives and collects EVE. WALL-E, determined to stay with her, becomes a stowaway. The spaceship carries them to an even larger spaceship named the *Axiom*. Once aboard the *Axiom*, WALL-E follows EVE to the bridge where she must deliver the plant. Captain McCrea is very excited to hear about the plant, but soon discovers that it is missing. WALL-E and EVE stumble across the plant, reclaim it, and head back to the Captain. Once they return to the bridge, the auto-pilot, named Auto, reveals he has been given special orders by the makers of the ship to never return to Earth due to it being inhospitable.

The Captain is outraged and points out the people who gave that order have been gone for centuries. Auto throws the plant away anyway and gets rid of WALL-E and EVE. WALL-E and EVE realize they must place the plant in the holo-detector, which will then put the ship on a direct course back to Earth. An injured WALL-E struggles to get the plant to the holo-detector while the Captain fights off Auto. The Captain eventually turns Auto off, which allows EVE to place the plant in the holo-detector. However, it is too late for WALL-E as he is badly damaged and almost completely ruined. As soon as the ship returns to Earth, EVE rushes straight to WALL-E's home, replaces his broken parts, and restores his memory. In the end, the humans realize they belong on Earth and begin to restore the world to its former glory.

Disney's Hollywood Studios

The only reference to the film can be found while riding the **Studio Backlot Tour**.

1) While riding the **Studio Backlot Tour**, you can find WALL-E himself on the left hand side of the tram as you pass the last window of the costuming building. Pay close attention as the tram usually goes past it fairly quickly so it is easy to miss.

Fun Fact: John Ratzenberger, who provides the voice of a character in every Pixar film, lent his voice to the character of John in WALL-E.

Index

Index key: DAK - Item is in Disney's Animal Kingdom
DHS - Item is in Disney's Hollywood Studios
DTD - Item is in Downtown Disney
E - Item is in Epcot
MK - Item is in Magic Kingdom
R - Item is in a resort

CPSIA information can be obtained at www.ICGtesting.com
Printed in the USA
LVOW082326250313

325975LV00001B/1/P